ESCAPING CAREER PRISON

THREE KEYS TO BREAKING FREE AND
FINDING WORK YOU LOVE

AMY VAN COURT

Published by Piaffe Press, LLC
Denver

Published by Piaffe Press, LLC
Denver, CO 80202

Publisher's Note
This publication is designed to provide accurate and authoritative informa-tion in regard to the subject matter covered. It is sold with the understand-ing that the publisher is not engaged in rendering psychological, financial, legal or other professional services. If expert assistance or counseling is needed, the services of a competent professional should be sought.

While the author has made every effort to provide accurate telephone numbers and Internet addresses at the time of publication, neither the publisher nor the author assumes any responsibility for errors, or for changes that occur after publication. Further, publisher does not have any control over and does not assume any responsibility for author or third-party Web sites or their content.

Visit our web site at www.escapingcareerprison.com

Allyson Peltier, Editor
Cover and interior design by Adina Cucicov, Flamingo Designs.
Cover image © Irochka—Fotolia.com
Author Photo by Havey Productions

ISBN: 978-0-9855566-1-7
Library of Congress Control Number: 2012908248

To you and your life in freedom

TABLE OF CONTENTS

NOTE TO THE READER

What This Book Is

I want to put myself out of work. The essential goal of my career guidance practice hasn't focused on the temporary—and recurring—nature of helping clients with résumés and cover letters, networking, and job boards. Instead, through coaching and public speaking I've sought to partner with women to help them gain the permanent gift of knowing themselves wholly and completely. So wholly and completely, in fact, that fluctuating career circumstances will have only a temporary effect on the quality of their lives.

Here's the thing: even after you land yourself in meaningful and fulfilling work, it's a certainty that your circumstances will change over time. You may move, get married, get unmarried, or have a child. Perhaps the wonderful career in which you find yourself—hopefully after doing the work this book asks of you—will evolve into something you hadn't planned on. The company you work for will change hands, Management will shift, clients will come and go. The likelihood that after you land your dream job you will spend your remaining working years in the same livelihood, with the same people, under the same circumstances, is essentially nil.

Bummer, huh?

But take heart, dear reader. Where you are now is a gift that can give you a lifetime of joy and wisdom. This can be the last time you find yourself lost, confused, unfulfilled, unhappy, and lacking confidence. With the help of this book, you will gain the ability to connect with the true, rooted part of yourself that doesn't change with your circumstances. This is the core of you, where you'll find love, compassion, acceptance, creativity and a deep knowing. I want you to know the path to the core of you so well that you can travel there any time you need or want to. You will become your own career (and life) counselor, and I will be happily out of a job.

After reading this book and committing to the exercises and resources it offers, you will have the necessary inner tools to adjust to any outer circumstance. Lucinda Miller, my career counselor in the late 1980s (they didn't have coaches back then), gave me the gift of being able to know who I truly am regardless of my circumstances, and I will be grateful to her forever. I continue to use many of the tools she gave me back then, and it's my wish to "pay it forward" to you through some of the exercises in this book. Since the time I worked with Lucinda, I have experienced

four—count 'em, four—career changes. Some were planned; some were not. Sometimes my work evolved from something I loved into something I didn't, without my realizing it until I was firmly planted in a place I didn't want to be. I was hired into big-title, high-paying jobs, some of which were deeply rewarding, while others sucked the life out of me. Along the way I also managed to demote myself into jobs that filled my heart with gladness. The circumstances changed. And every dot led to another, though of course I didn't see those connections at the time.

> *(Y)ou can't connect the dots looking forward; you can only connect them looking backward. So you have to trust that the dots will somehow connect in your future. You have to trust in something—your gut, destiny, life, karma, whatever. This approach has never let me down, and it has made all the difference in my life.*
>
> **Steve Jobs**

All of those career dots connected to this place, where I am now. My work, my purpose here on this spinning blue ball, is to give you what Lucinda Miller gave to me: the ability to return to *who you are*, regardless of (and perhaps in spite of) your circumstances. With knowledge and acceptance of yourself, you will have the resources, tools and support to create anything in this life that you desire, including a career that is deeply rewarding and fulfilling. If you've been looking "out there" for the answers, dear reader, it's time to change your focus and widen the lens for a bigger view. The answers, recognition, support and compassion you have been seeking are in the vast place inside you. They've always

been there and no matter what happens along the way, they're never leaving. *You* are the expert you've been seeking; it's my job and my privilege to show you how to access your inner expert consistently and reliably, whenever you need it.

I find it fascinating, and a delicious example of the universe's humor, that our eyes are on the outside of our bodies. We habitually look away from ourselves for support and answers; it's why you're reading this book, right?

Please believe this: whether you're ecstatic or miserable, fulfilled or empty, where you really need to look first—for all the beauty and strength, love and validation you will ever need—is *inside*. You carry your greatest hope, compassion, support and love with you always. You don't have to go get it. It's not necessary to wait for it or to rely on someone else to provide it. It's already inside you in every single moment, waiting to be tapped. Isn't that amazing?

> *The Creator gathers all the animals and says: "I want to hide something from humans until they are ready for it: the realization that they create their own reality."*
>
> *"Give it to me. I'll fly it to the moon," says the eagle.*
>
> *"No, one day soon they will go there and find it."*
>
> *"How about the bottom of the ocean?" asks the salmon.*

"No, they will find it there too."

"I will bury it in the great plains," says the buffalo.

"They will soon dig and find it there."

"Put it inside them," says the wise grandmother mole.

"Done," says the Creator." It is the last place they will look."

Native American parable

I wrote *Escaping Career Prison* after years of helping women free themselves from unfulfilling work and, in doing so, land in livelihoods that allow them to be who they are and to make a difference in the world that only they can make. A meaningful career is the result of introspection and embracing one's self deeply, and often in a brand-new way. The aim of this book is to provide you with the understanding and tools that my clients have used to gain their own career happiness and freedom. Accompanying smart and determined women on their very personal journeys toward career success, and being there in the joyous moment when they land in the work that lights them up inside, is my life's mission and passion. I want you to feel the same personal and professional delight in your career that I do in mine. I believe passionately that knowing ourselves and putting our unique traits, passions and talents to use for the benefit of others is why we're here on earth.

Escaping Career Prison will help you get to know yourself—maybe in a completely new way—and move forward with the confidence that comes from self-knowledge and self-acceptance. The authentic, powerful truth of you is ready to break open the gates into the career freedom and fulfillment that only you can create. I can't do it for you, and I am delighted to be here to guide and support you.

> *You have to do it by yourself. And you can't do it alone.*
> **Martin Rutte**

View this book as a toolkit designed to help you find and live the answers that reside within you. My role is to be your mirror and your guide: I will help you see yourself authentically so the unique and resonant path to your career fulfillment will become clear. I will also be your own personal Google, providing you with "search results" intended to inform, motivate, and inspire you toward your life's calling.

What This Book Is Not

Escaping Career Prison is not intended to help you go about the business of finding a job. It is a book designed to help you go about the business of finding YOU. If you're looking for help with a résumé or cover letter, or how to interview, or how to find the right test to take so you'll know exactly what you "should" be doing, this is not the book for you. And if you've gone down that road of résumés, cover letters, job boards, and so on before, and now find yourself back here, feeling lost, confused, and perhaps scared and frustrated, isn't it time to ask if perhaps the way

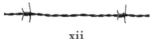

you've gone about finding your ideal work in the past may not be the best plan going forward?

We cannot continue to do things the same way and expect a different result.

There is a place for the to-do list that includes résumés and interviewing techniques. It comes *after* you find and free yourself. *You will not learn who you are by putting together and sending out a résumé.* Please, do yourself and the world a tremendous favor: invest in finding your unique self and what you were born to do *first*. Venture inside yourself for the answers and take the leap of faith to believe that once you know yourself, the to-do list will make a lot more sense.

INTRODUCTION

If you've picked up this book, chances are you're feeling stuck. Stuck in work that is unfulfilling at best and soul-sucking at worst. You may be experiencing a general malaise, a "divine discomfort" that feels like an uneasy tapping on the shoulder of your conscience, or you may be in a flat-out panic, struggling to resist taking any job, anywhere, just to get out of the hell you're in now. Or perhaps you're feeling completely paralyzed, and ideas of what to do and where to go are as absent as snow in the Sahara. The questions, oh the questions that swirl in your mind:

"What should I do?"

"How do I get out of here?"

"What's next?"

"It's been so long since I felt passionate about work, am I even capable of passion anymore?"

"What if there's something wrong with me and I'm not meant for joy-filled work?"

You probably don't trust yourself with a decision as important as what career to choose next. I mean, really: your best choices got you here, and here's not so good!

Then there are those times when you just think,

"Hey, today wasn't so bad. Maybe this is all there is. Maybe no one really loves their job and fulfilling work is just a fantasy, as rare as winning the lottery. I should be grateful to have this job, or any job for that matter. Perhaps I should just stick it out; something will change eventually. I suppose I could get used to this—it *is* a paycheck, after all."

And then your soul cries out:

"This is not me. I don't belong here! Not another day, not another minute! I don't know what I dreamed of, but this is surely not it."

Feel that feeling in you. Feel that sense of unease, of jittery-jaggedness and a pulling on your cells. Is it hard to be still in your body? Is there a low-grade (or perhaps not-so-low-grade) indescribable fear occupying your thoughts, bones and muscles, and everything in between?

Welcome to Career Prison.

You have been serving time for a crime you didn't commit. The sentence is harsh and the way out is unclear. You're suffocating in here; fresh air and freedom are distant memories. Ideas about

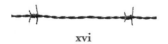

how to get out, and what life could look like if you do, are out of reach. And then there's that paralyzing question, the one that keeps you firmly planted in this prison cell where you are small, life is small, and realized dreams are the property of people more deserving, worthy, special, lucky, or (fill in the blank) than you. You know that question:

What if I fail?

And what a question it is! Can you feel how it stops the dream dead in its tracks? Literally, dead in its tracks. For you and many others just like you, there lives a teeny sliver of hope, a small seed of optimism that things will change. But a failed effort, well, that would kill that seed of hope once and for all. You would become A Lifer. So in this perverse way, you have found a way to keep hope alive through fear of failure. Your brilliant brain, as Prison Warden, has so thoroughly twisted your existence that staying in Career Prison actually feels safer than breaking out! Can you see, can you *feel* how backward that thinking is? And that's what happens when we spend so much time in captivity, without the freedom to be who we are and to do work that allows—even requires—our magic and our unique gifts to play with wild abandon.

So. Four things:
1. You don't deserve to be here.
2. You've done nothing wrong.
3. You are innocent of all crimes and you've been falsely convicted.
4. The only failure is the failure to try.

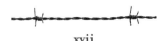

This book is a journey that will deliver sweet rewards along the way and by the end, a resonant vision of who you are and the kind of career that will light you up. But you have to do the meaningful *inner* work this book requires in order to land in meaningful *outer* work. You are being asked to travel deep inside yourself to connect with what's there and report back. Do the exercises. Check out the resources. Engage. Don't "phone it in." You will receive from this process what you give to it. And it's not just about doing the work, it's about being curious and growing from it. You must be invested in finding your own answers. You must break the bad habit of looking to others, whether they're experts or not, for the truth and direction that only you can know. If it will serve you, ask a friend to hold you accountable to this process. Heck, you can ask me to hold you accountable if that's what it will take. Just e-mail me at **amy@ possibilitiesunlimited.org** and tell me how you want to be held accountable, and (within reason) I'll do it. It means that much to me. No matter what, please honor your heart's longing for a richly satisfying and passion-filled livelihood. When you do, the world can't help but benefit.

Okay, let's get you out. Right now.

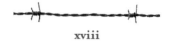

THE KEY RING:
WHAT HOLDS IT ALL TOGETHER

Disenchantment, whether it is a minor disappointment or a major shock, is the signal that things are moving into transition in our lives.

William Bridges

When you finish this book you will have Three Keys. They are good ones, simple (though not always easy) and effective. They will get you out, that's for sure. And they need a Key Ring—something to hold them, and to hold you, while you journey out into the vast wildlands of fulfilling new work. It is the crucial element that will help you unlock the prison gates and break free into the wide open land of career freedom. The Key Ring that holds it all together is this: Stay.

"STAY?!" you exclaim. *"I want to get out and I want out now! You're giving me the Three Keys to career freedom and you want me to STAY?!"*

So just hang on a minute and I'll explain. In his book *Transitions*, William Bridges explores the three stages in any change: The Ending, The Beginning, and the place where The Ending has ended but The Beginning hasn't yet begun. This third place is called The Neutral Zone. It is the hardest, scariest, most uncomfortable and challenging place you can be. It's also the richest, most important soil in the becoming of who you are. There's a very good chance you're there now.

When we're in The Neutral Zone, we want to escape the discomfort, the gritchy not-knowingness of it. Answers don't live on the surface of The Neutral Zone; they aren't easily found. But they are there, trust me. They're deep inside. And the answers you'll find aren't about what you should Do, they are about who you Are. You'll encounter your courage here; your soul, your spirit, your hope and despair are here. YOU are here.

Before a caterpillar can become a butterfly, it must spend some quality time in The Neutral Zone, what we call the chrysalis. There it is in there, neither caterpillar nor winged beauty; instead it's probably something akin to primordial mush. No legs, eyes, antennae, or wings, just goop. I've never interviewed a butterfly so I don't know this for sure, but I'm willing to bet it didn't know how long it would take to become a butterfly or what it should Do to get out. It just stayed in that dark place because it was the only way the old parts could disintegrate and

the new ones could be born. It just simply can't be having a good time in there!

What's worse for the butterfly is that if a chrysalis is opened too soon, the whole thing dies. No second chances when rushing the mush. But if you or I hurry our chrysalis-stage process along, the worst that can happen is a return to caterpillar-dom and then back to the chrysalis again. It's not death, but seriously: do you want to return to mushy, gooey darkness when freedom is within your grasp?

The goal of course is progress, and I'm asking you to redefine *progress* so that you will understand that "staying" in the unknown is sometimes the only way that moving forward can eventually happen.

If you scamper through the discomfort of The Neutral Zone, perhaps as you always have, you will create the same old results. Do you want to escape Career Prison for real, and for good, or do you just want a Day Pass? A Day Pass is temporary distraction from the truth, from the real work at hand. I do not recommend the Day Pass when permanent escape is within your reach—like a Brass Ring. Get it?

So instead of rushing through or skipping over The Neutral Zone to more familiar, less soupy, dark, and uncomfortable territory, please be willing to Stay. For a while. For how long? I don't know. But if you Stay long enough, you will know when it's time to go. You'll feel a longing instead of a grasping. You'll

want to move toward something instead of away from something. There will be a resonant readiness inside you; an energy that wants to create, whereas before you were reacting. And most of all, you will believe in yourself, with the certainty that a career that will bring you joy, one that feels uniquely like YOU, is your birthright. You'll feel it's out there, waiting for you to claim it.

By the way, Staying is not the same thing as Waiting. Waiting, as we will explore in Key Number Two, is a Prison Warden delay tactic intended to keep you stuck. Ducks must be nicely lined up in a row; all the "what if" questions must be answered. Waiting implies that something "out there" must happen in order for you to feel "safe" and comfortable in moving forward. Staying, on the other hand, is the practice of exploring inside yourself first and going forward from a place of knowing who you are, even when the ducks aren't in single file, it's uncomfortable, and you don't have all the answers.

> *You may think you have to have all the answers for you to be at peace. But the truth is, answers don't bring you peace. You have to settle down into the scrappy, unknown ride and hold your own hand. Make peace with unanswerable questions and no guarantees. Peace brings you answers.*
>
> **Tama Kieves**

Like a key ring, these intentions must be held close to you at all times in order for the keys to be accessible and effective:

- Be willing to "be still and know" yourself. Invest in yourself by learning who you are at your core. Notice yourself regularly, as if you're a separate entity observing the person who is You. Learn everything there is to know about you. Embrace yourself. Smile at your foibles, your floppy awkwardness, your strength and vulnerability. Accept all of you. Be curious in the space of you. Accept that you are not your consequences and your consequences are not you.

- Avoid the hamster wheel. Your Prison Warden knows that if you are busy on the wheel, where you can run hard and go nowhere, you will not be in a position to make big, meaningful change. Are you hearing an insistent, panicked voice that says *"What are you going to DO?! You're not DOING anything! Get up! Go out! Perfect your résumé! Send it like wallpaper samples to every office in town!"* Yep, your Warden wants you to be busy *doing* stuff to keep you from being still, *knowing* stuff. Resist the urge to "just do something" and wait until the Doing has Meaning. It will happen, if you will just be courageous enough to stay awake to yourself and Be.

- Explore ways to commune with your Wisdom. Commit to being with her, tuning in to her, and trusting her. Your Prison Warden is alive and well in stories about your past and future. Your Wisdom lives in the present. In The Now. Be willing to be present, through creative acts like painting, pottery, music, and writing; through natural/physical experiences like walking in the woods or along the beach;

and through meditation where you and your Wisdom can sit together and observe you. The two of you will notice your thoughts pass by like clouds on the sky of you. When you realize that you are not your thoughts and your thoughts are not you, you can choose the ones that serve you and let the others go.

Stay, dear reader. For just a while. Turn your awareness to the in-between place; the place in each blink where your eyelid is neither going up nor going down. That split second when your lungs are neither expanding nor contracting. Be there for a while. Get to know the part of you that is timeless, unaffected by circumstances, pure and whole. Use the exercises offered in this book. Get to know yourself newly. Dream in Technicolor. Immerse yourself in the river of your life experience—feel the water on your skin, notice the current. Is the bottom sandy or slippery? Rocky perhaps? Or maybe you can't feel the bottom. It's all good, because you're in it. Be in it for a while, if you're willing. Don't wait, but do Stay.

THE FIRST KEY:
START WHERE YOU ARE

Here you are in prison, wondering how you got here and what it will take to get out. It's a place with so many more questions than answers, isn't it? Well, settle in for just a bit (a short bit, I promise) and let's talk about spiritual mysticism.

"WHAT?!" you say. "I have no time for this. I'm in hell and if I can't figure out how to get out soon, I may sink into an even deeper despair and never find my way to escape."

To escape Career Prison and land in a career that brings you fulfillment, joy and satisfaction, you must first embrace a simple, age-old, three-word concept:

Being, Doing, Having.

In that order.

The spiritual community has long believed in this idea, and you may just become a believer too. Here's how it applies to you.

First, Know thyself. This ancient Greek aphorism was inscribed on a wall in the Temple of Apollo at Delphi. It dates back to the fourth century B.C. Clearly, *Know thyself* is not a new concept. And yet, when I begin working with a client, nearly 100 percent of the time the first question I ask is one she can't answer.

I ask her to tell me who she is.

Not what she does, not what she's good at or what other people say about her. I want to know Who She Is. Typically this question produces a long pause and then shortly thereafter, the reply, "That's a hard question. I don't have any idea. What do you mean?" And that's when I know we're about to begin a beautiful journey of Discovery.

You see, what the mystics knew, and what I want you to know, is that it all must begin with who you are. Who you are Being.

Second, Do in a way that expresses the truth of who you Are. Your unique gifts, perspective, and energy are in you for a reason: to express themselves out in the world for the good of yourself and others. Only you have the gifts you have, in the combination and amounts present. When what you Do is a reflection of those gifts, the world is whole and so are you. Without the expression of your uniqueness, the world is missing an important, let's even say world-changing element. In order for the world to be whole,

and for you to feel your wholeness, you must Do work that allows who you are to Be present in great measure.

> *The grace of God means something like: Here is your life. You might never have been, but you are because the party wouldn't have been complete without you.*
> **Frederick Buechner**

Third, when we are clear on who we are Being, and we Do from that place, the Having part just seems to take care of itself. Having includes the money, the car, the house, the commute, the job title, the relationships, and so on.

Let me say this again: When we Do as an expression of who we uniquely Are, the Having part will naturally come about. This is what we call *flow*.

So are you ready to be let off the hook a little bit?

Here goes.

Where you are in your career is not your fault.

In our Western culture, most of us learn to begin the job/career search at the Doing or Having stage. We ask ourselves, "What am I good at?" or "What kind of experience do I have?" or "What can I put on my résumé that will get me that job?" Perhaps we tailor ourselves to the available job openings. Or we begin with "I need X dollars per year in salary," or "I want to

buy a house in such-and-such neighborhood," or "If I don't get the title of vice president, I'm not going to take the job."

What's most beautifully fascinating about this is that the universe will often grant us those wishes. If we are persistent, we find work that fits with our past experience. We get the salary we want and the job title that communicates our position and reflects our skills. Ever heard the expression "Be careful what you wish for"? Uh-huh.

We get what we wish for and then, ultimately, we find ourselves in Career Prison, scratching our noggins and wondering what the hell happened.

Tama Kieves, a wonderful author and coach who has inspired many, many people with her work and her book *This Time I Dance! Creating the Work You Love*, tells of the time she was smack-dab in the hell of a Career Prison that from the outside looked to many like "success." She had graduated from Harvard Law School and was a highly paid attorney at a top law firm in Denver. She was "successful" by all accounts. She was making good money; she was well respected. Her family and friends were pleased.

One small problem: she was dying inside. All of the Doing had been done, and done well. She might have justified remaining in Career Prison because she was Doing a great job. And in the middle of a hell that can genuinely mean the end of life for some, grace appeared in the comment made by a friend:

"If you're this successful doing work you don't *love, what could you do with work you* do *love?"*

So take heart: whether you're doing well where you are or not, the sense you're experiencing that something is missing is real. It's a cosmic shoulder tap that can become a two-by-four to the forehead when ignored. As a good friend once told me, *"The universe keeps getting a bigger hammer until it gets your attention."* Work that does not allow us to express who we are, no matter how well it pays or how busy and important we seem, is unfulfilling and empty. Period. You are not here to make a lot of money or have a fancy job title. Or even to work really, really hard and retire with a full retirement fund and an empty heart. You are here to make your unique mark on the world, in the way that only you can.

> *Don't ask what the world needs. Ask what makes you come alive, and go do it. Because what the world needs is people who have come alive.*
>
> **Howard Thurman**

Good Days and Bad Days

When I was a little girl we used to gather at the supper table at six P.M. every evening. One night after returning from a business trip, my dad told us of his experience touring a manufacturing plant. This particular factory produced canned pork and beans (hey, it's got to come from somewhere, doesn't it?). Anyway, while walking through the plant, Dad came upon a man whose sole function in the process was the final touch of placing one square of pork on top of the beans before the lid was sealed on

the can. This fascinated my dad—not so much the actual process, but the fact that a person did this all day long for a living. So he began asking the man about his job.

> *"How do you like your job?"* inquired my dad.
> *"It's okay,"* replied the man.
> Dad: *"How long have you been doing this?"*
> Man: *"Oh, about seven years."*

(*Seven years???*) At this point my dad, who is an inherently curious person, became even more intrigued by this factory worker. After all, how often does one encounter a person willing to perform such a repetitive and seemingly uninteresting job for so long? What makes a person like that tick? What would keep him in that job? And so Dad asked:

> *"I'm wondering, sir: How do you tell the good days from the bad days?"*

Honestly, I don't remember the man's answer. Or even if he had an answer. I don't even know if my dad intended to make this a teaching moment for his little girl at the dinner table or if it was simply a story of a day in his career. But what I took from that story was a profound and enduring lesson that informed and affected the rest of my life. I received the gift of learning that work—and life—wasn't about expecting only the good and avoiding the bad. It was about knowing the difference between the two. Every single day. A fulfilling career isn't one with no bad days; it is one that offers good and bad days and, most important of all, the ability to be who we are regardless of the kind of day we're having.

Are you having a bad day, a bad job, or a bad career? The only way to truly know the difference, and to have more good ones, is to know yourself.

Your Values

As I said a page or two ago, knowing who you are is the first, the most important, and, for some people, the most delicious step toward career fulfillment. You have a unique combination of traits and characteristics that sets you apart from every other being on the planet. I call these characteristics your Values. Consider your fingerprints, for example; no one has a fingerprint just like yours. Just as your fingerprints were designed to leave a mark on the world that is unique to you, the same can be said for your Values.

So what are your unique Values? Before we delve into that, let's get clear on what Values are not. Values are not morals. There are no right or wrong Values. There is no judgment inherent in Values. For example, I prefer dark chocolate. Perhaps you prefer potato chips. No one is wrong here, we're just different. Same goes for all Values, though often in our humanness we attach judgment to them. We may choose to believe that a person with a value of *finishing early* is "better" than someone who *procrastinates.* If you're someone who has made the choice to believe that, that's fine. However, the next time you need the services of someone who operates well under pressure, who is great at handling unanticipated speed bumps and pulling things together at the last minute, and who honors deadlines, you may do well to consider a procrastinator. They tend to be creative, think fast on their feet, and get things done. They may not real-

ize it, but they procrastinate because doing so allows them to put their unique talents and skills to use.

> *Be yourself; everyone else is already taken.*
>
> **Oscar Wilde**

At the end of this chapter, you'll find a great exercise called "Your Values Map" that will help you determine your values and identify the degree to which you're currently living them. Now's a good time to head on over to your first important task. Give it a go. I'll wait here.

The Three Questions

> *When Doing becomes infused with the timeless quality of Being, that is success.*
>
> **Eckhart Tolle**

Now that you've explored and identified your Values, what do you Do with that information?

There are three crucial questions to ask yourself any time you're contemplating a new job or career, or even whether to stay where you are. All three of these questions must be answered in the affirmative if you are to land in fulfilling work that has meaning to you:

1. *Will this job/career allow me to bring who I am to work every day?* This is the essence of the matter; can you work your val-

ues in this position? If the answer is No, then for heaven's sake, keep looking. If the answer is Yes, then HOORAY! And on to the next question:

2. *Does the organization I am/will be working in support and share my values?* By *organization* I mean the company culture, senior management, and so on. Think of this as the people who have a say in your success (with a small *s*): the folks who have a say in your income, raises, promotions, performance evaluations. It is crucial to be working somewhere that recognizes and rewards your values. When you do, you feel seen, understood, appreciated, and challenged. When you don't, it can really, really be a fruitless, stressful, and soul-sucking experience. An important note here: if you're working somewhere that doesn't share your values, no one is wrong. See the preceding definition of Values: they don't inherently contain judgment.

Here's an example: if you have a strong value around cultivating deep connections with people, you may have worked hard to become the "go-to person" for your clients. They love you, they trust you, they rely on you to look after their best interests. You believe in your heart of hearts that the long-term benefit your company gains from this relationship is high. However, if you work for an organization that has strong values around selling as many "units" *now* to as many clients as possible, you may find yourself at cross-purposes. In your employer's perspective, you're falling down on the job of selling what

needs to be sold in high quantities *today*. In your perspective, you're cultivating a relationship that will result in longevity and long-term sales. No one is wrong here. Your employer has every right to value immediate unit sales. And you have every right to value long-term, trusting relationships with your clients. Ideally you may be able to find a middle ground that works for both of you. If not, what's best to take away from this situation is simply this: it's a poor values fit.

Okay! So let's say the question of whether the organization shares and supports your values can also been answered in the affirmative. YIPPEE!! On to Question 3.

3. *Do the people with whom I rub elbows—my colleagues, co-workers, peers—also share my values?* If so, then you are in what I call your Work Tribe. An affirmative answer to this question is every bit as important as the answers to Questions 1 and 2, and I can't tell you how often it's overlooked. When you're working with your Tribe, everyone makes everyone better. The bar is raised in a delicious, meaningful, and resonant way. It's not only safer to make mistakes, take risks, and fail, it's also safer to succeed. Your Work Tribe enfolds and encourages you. They "get" you at a level far deeper than the Doing place. They experience you from the Being place. They will cheer you on, celebrate your wins, and demonstrate compassion (and learning) around your mistakes. They will be your water when you're having a desert day. They encourage, challenge, and accept

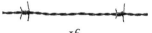

you. They bring you into the fold because the Tribe feels more complete with you in it. A Work Tribe is a beautiful, magnificent, magical thing. You need one.

Here's a bit of a generalization that still rings true for those who have heard it: We have grown up in a culture that teaches women to hold a different perspective than men when something is amiss. When a woman tries on clothing that doesn't fit, she tends to say things like, "My butt's too big," "My breasts are too small," or something similar. She puts the clothes back on the rack and walks away believing that she is the problem.

A man, on the other hand, has grown up in a culture where if the suit doesn't fit, he gets it tailored. If the pant legs are too long, he has them shortened. If the waist is too tight, he has it let out. It isn't about what needs to be different about him, it's about what needs to be different about the suit. Work that doesn't allow you to be who you are is like a suit that doesn't fit. It's not the suit's fault and it's not your fault. It's simply a bad fit. No matter how fancy the suit is, or how hard you work in it, it's still a bad fit. Blaming the suit or yourself is wasted energy—it won't get you out of the suit and into one that fits beautifully.

However, unlike suits, jobs are difficult to alter. Chances are if it's a bad fit today, it's not going to become a better fit tomorrow. Your employer and your co-workers have as much right to their values as you do to yours. No one gets to be wrong here. If the work doesn't fit you, it is up to you to find new work. Buying a suit that turns out to be too small is bad enough. But choosing

to keep it and wear it, when it gets in the way of your freedom of movement and kills your confidence, is just plain nutty. You are going to find work that fits you beautifully. And when you do, you will be able to stretch and grow and Be and Do in something that supports who you Are. And you'll look great too!

> *You are not here merely to make a living. You are here in order to enable the world to live more amply, with greater vision, with a finer spirit of hope and achievement. You are here to enrich the world, and you impoverish yourself when you forget the errand.*
>
> **Woodrow Wilson**

FIRST KEY EXERCISES

As you probably know, putting writing exercises inside a book can present a challenge because some people would rather not write in a book, or they are borrowing a book that has already been written in. Happily, I hold a big value around detail and providing convenience for others, so I'm providing you with an option to make your experience with this book as easy and meaningful as possible.

If you'd prefer to have all of the book's exercises printed out so they're physically separate from the reading material and you can complete them on paper, I've provided that option for you free of charge. Simply go to the following link on my web site, where you can download the *Escaping Career Prison Workbook*: www.escapingcareerprison.com/workbook.

EXERCISE ONE:
YOUR VALUES MAP

At the end of this exercise you'll find an extensive list of Values. You're going to use the Values on this list, and add some of your own, to create a customized map of who you Are.

Step 1: Find a quiet place with no distractions where you have the freedom to look inside yourself and notice who you truly are. Get centered, whatever that means for you. You can close your eyes and take a few deep breaths, light a candle, put on some soothing music, or make a nice cup of tea—whatever helps you "be present" and leave the stories and distractions of your day behind.

Step 2: From the list, identify each Value that you know is either inherent in you or something you value in your life. Aim for a minimum of 30 to 40 identified Values. They should encompass your whole self and not be limited only to your work self. While it may not be possible to live certain Values in your work day, you most definitely want work that will give you the freedom to honor those values outside of work.

Step 3: Now we're going to create a Values Map. Using the form provided on the Worksheet (www.escapingcareerprison.com/workbook) or on a blank page (or two or three), draw three columns. The first column will be the widest; write the heading "Value" at the top and transcribe your checked Values from the list. The second and third columns only need to be wide enough to accommodate a two-digit number. Write the heading "Importance" over the second column and "Degree I'm Living It" over the third.

Go ahead and complete these steps before continuing.

Step 4: While the list I gave you to identify your Values is extensive, it may not be 100 percent complete. You probably have Values that aren't on the list. Take a few moments to observe yourself again—you can pretend you are a separate person who is noticing You, the first person—and come up with any additional Values that are true for You but not on the list. Add those to your new three-column Values Map.

Step 5: Now look at each Value on your three-column list individually. For each Value, identify its importance to you on a scale of 0 to 10, with a score of 0 meaning it's not important at all and 10 meaning it is extremely important. There is no rule about how many 10s—or 9s or any other number—you can have. Once you're finished, if you find that any Value has a score less than 5, which isn't very strong, take it off the list. It is crucial that you get out of your head and feel (rather than analyze) your answers. If you find you're struggling for a number, you're most definitely in your head. Shift your attention to your body and go with your gut.

Step 6: Next, place a number from 0 to 10 in the third "Degree I'm Living It" column, with 0 meaning you're not living it at all and 10 meaning you're living it fully.

Remember, this Values Map is yours; it's about you, so let go of any "shoulds" or other judgments related to your Values. This exercise is about knowing and embracing yourself fully. Judgments about what you should or shouldn't have as a Value, or the degree to which you should or shouldn't be living it, won't serve you. You have the power to let judgment go; I suggest you do just that.

Step 7: After you've filled in all the numbers for your Values, notice those where there is a gap between the first number and the second. HINT: "Importance" is a Being number, while "Living" is a Doing number. So if you are someone who values Being Creative at a 9 and you're living that Value at a 4, that's a five-point gap; you're likely feeling out of balance and "not yourself" in this area of your life. Conversely, if you value something at an 8 and you're living it at an 8, you probably feel in alignment in that area of your life/career.

TA-DA! Now you have a complete map (a snapshot of this moment in time) of your Values. You can see what's working and what's missing where you are now. This matters! Your Values Map will evolve with time; ideally the gap between numbers for each Value will get smaller as you make important career and life changes. From now on, you can use this Map to identify the following:

- Who you are and what needs to be present in your work
- Whether a prospective employer will be a good fit with what's important to you
- The characteristics of your Tribe so you'll know them when you see them

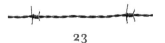

Bonus Step: It probably won't be possible to bring 100 percent of your Values to work each day. Some Values aren't directly related to your career (such as being married or being a great daughter). Go back through your list and identify the values that absolutely must be embraced and supported in your work. Is there a big gap between the "Importance" and "Living" numbers for those? What does this tell you about why you feel imprisoned now? How does it inform your priority-setting for the next job?

Many of my clients have started new careers or taken/not taken jobs based on their Values Map alone. This is the most important consideration for any career decision you make going forward. Your Values Map will guide you to fulfilling work that allows and encourages you to be who you are in the work that you do.

Suggestion: Update this Values Map every four to six months. Go back and revisit and identify where you've closed the gap between "Importance" and "Living." Maybe you'll find that something you believed was a 10 in importance is now an 8—your Warden was telling you it "should" be very important to you and now you're willing to accept that, in truth, it's just not. And more commonly, you'll see where you've made huge strides in the "Living" number and where your attention is needed. I hope that after doing the Values Map exercise and completing this book, you will be pleasantly surprised every time you check in with it.

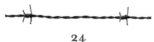

List of Values for Exercise One

Being vulnerable
Being determined
Being a communicator
Being assertive
Being organized
Being punctual
Being a sounding board
Being a "go-to person"
Being inclusive/open-minded/
  tolerant
Variety
Freedom
Being introspective/self aware
Being supportive
Being nurturing
Being persistent
Being a collaborator
Being spiritual
Being a great friend
Being known for doing something
  well
Being grounded/down to earth
Making a difference
Being someone who makes an impact
Being challenged
Setting and achieving goals
Being responsible
Being outside my comfort zone
Being independent
Being in love
Personal growth
Being a writer
Giving back
Being financially free
Being accountable
Being "in the river" of my life (vs. on

the bank)
Being prepared
Being in my own company
Being cautious
Being thorough
Being courageous
Being analytical
Surpassing expectations
Integrity
Being honest/trustworthy
Being a problem solver
Being loyal
Helping others live better lives
Being physically active
Having a vision for my life
Being seen/understood/heard
Being passionate about something
Being confident
Being professional
Being productive
Faith
Being "on purpose"
Believing in a higher power
Being positive/an optimist
Being open
Being unconventional/outside the
  box
Connecting deeply with others
Being empathetic
Being tenacious
Discovery/uncovering new things
Sharing my knowledge or experience
  for the benefit of others
Being at peace
Being authentic/"real"/transparent
Overcoming obstacles

Being someone who keeps
commitments
Being in meaningful relationships
Being respected
Being focused
Being part of a support network/
Tribe
Living in the flow
Being someone who follows through
Being playful
Living a fulfilling life
Being curious
Being specific
Being comfortable
Being around interesting people
Being inspired
Being someone who inspires others
Humor/wit
Sense of humanity
Being compassionate/kind
Being a mom
Being well known/recognized/
famous
Being happily married
Being around other creative people
Being a champion/advocate for
others
Being a dancer
Being generous
Being charitable
Being an entrepreneurial spirit
Friendship
Being empowered/powerful
Being strong
Following my passion
Being a dreamer
Being smart
Being a loving person

Self-love
Being articulate
Being someone who expresses her
feelings
Being successful
Being an artist
Seeing the bigger picture
Self-care
Being in nature/outdoors
Being a planner
Being in the presence of beauty
Having memorable experiences
Having deep, close friendships
Being boisterous
Being outrageous
Being fair
Being attractive
Being healthy
Being fit
Reading and books
Being flexible
Balance
Travel/adventure
Fun
Having a plan
Being quick-witted
Being creative
Being methodical
Being funny/making people laugh
Being unfiltered
Being relied on
Helping others grow and succeed
Being an expert at something
Experiencing new cultures
Being fiscally responsible
Achieving something important and/
or difficult
Living my potential

Making a positive impact on others
Being my own person
Being a risk taker
Being a priority in my life
Clarity
Change
Being committed
Being social
Being in an intimate relationship
Being in a community with exceptional people
Living in the moment
Being direct/to the point
Being grateful
Creating welcoming and inviting spaces for others
Leading the charge
Researching things that interest me
Being true to self
Family
Being a powerhouse
Being financially secure
Being adventurous/exploring
Being spontaneous
Living a full life
Being someone with no regrets
Being a trail blazer
A sense of community/belonging/being part of something
Learning
Helping those less fortunate
Presenting myself well
Being happy
Being patient
Being relaxed/at ease/easygoing
Being in a successful marriage
Being intellectually challenged
Making things happen

Being CEO of my life/taking ownership
Being hopeful
Being part of something bigger
Getting to the heart of the matter
Being a good partner
Animals
Looking good
Being someone who gets things done
Being resilient
Being unstoppable
Exploring possibilities
Being considerate/polite
Being intuitive
Solitude
Self-sufficient
Being matter-of-fact
Being a calm influence
Achieving something meaningful
Being part of a team
Being a role model
Making sense of complex things
Using my gifts for the benefit of others
Being a great sister
Being driven
Fashion
Resolving social injustice
Making things better
Being effective
Being motivated/Having a fire in the belly
Motivating others
Being objective/Seeing other perspectives
Being a mentor

Exercise Two:
Your Success Map

All your life, the universe has been dropping bread crumbs disguised as experiences. For as far back as you can remember, starting with when you were a wee one, you have enjoyed experiences where you felt most alive, most successful, most "in the flow" of your life. Think of them as bread crumbs. The past experiences that struck a resonant chord in you contain important elements that, if lived again, will strike the same harmonious response in you. This exercise is both a complement to and a departure from your Values Map; it's designed to use your past to help identify the experiences and parts of you that need to be present for you to feel joyful, fulfilled, and deeply satisfied with yourself and your life. From those moments you will identify the key elements. And across the key elements you will see a pattern, a trail of meaning that will guide you to more of the same.

Step 1: Divide your life into decades: 0 to 10 years old, 11 to 20, 21 to 30, and so on. Within each decade, identify at least three times when you felt successful, alive, joyous, and fully yourself. Maybe these were times when you had an intuitive sense of being aligned with the exact reasons why you are in the world, when you celebrated an achievement or just felt grateful and delighted to be alive. *These times do not need to be career-oriented.*

Selecting these experiences intuitively is important because you may not be able to articulate rationally why you felt on purpose/successful/grateful during this time. Going back to your childhood can be helpful; you may find clues from a time in your life when the opinions of others and your analytical mind didn't come into play. It will help to start your list quickly and not to analyze why certain things are on the list.

Step 2: Now go back and write briefly about each experience. For each one, write about what you did, where you were, what the outcome was, and how you felt. Deeply immerse yourself in what it was like to be you at that time. For each experience, answer these questions:

- What was essential to my sense of fulfillment in this experience?
- What did I learn about myself?
- What choices did I make?
- Who was I being?

Step 3: After you've written about all of your experiences, go back and highlight the key words from each one. Key words are those that feel meaningful/resonant to you and those that appear often. Then copy the highlighted words from your experiences onto a separate page.

Now examine the key words to identify the commonalities and themes, appearing like bright neon arrows pointing toward what fulfills you in life. They are guiding you toward a career that will light up your soul by allowing you to be who you truly are and to impact the world in the way only you can.

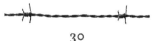

Exercise Three:
Your Purpose Statement

Your Success Map is showing you more than what fulfills you; it's pointing out why you're here on earth. It's no accident that what's deeply satisfying and meaningful to you is also your gift to others. Now draft a brief statement of your life purpose in two to four sentences using the key words and phrases from your Success Map. Every person has a unique purpose, so no two are alike and there are no "wrong" Purpose Statements. However, it may help get your creative juices flowing to see a couple of examples:

- "The purpose of my life is to create a world of love and empowerment, by loving and empowering myself and others."

- "My purpose is to work generously and to live in service; to manifest love through connecting with myself and others; and to support the development of wisdom and peace in myself, my colleagues, my clients and my community."

Another perspective on creating your life Purpose Statement is to use metaphor. The structure might look something like this:

"I am the _____ _____ that _____
so that _____."

Examples:

- "I am the harbor light that shows the way in the fog so others may return home."
- "I am the aspen tree that changes with the seasons to live a strong and flexible life."
- "I am the locksmith who opens doors and gives freedom to others."
- "I am the uncut diamond that shines from within. My beauty and strength are unchanged by the circumstances around me."

Don't expect to get it right in an hour; this is your first draft. Let it "simmer" inside you for several days and tweak it as new thoughts and ideas come up. Play with it, add stuff, scratch stuff out. It may grow long and you'll need to edit, combine, cut. What you're after is the heart of the matter, the essence; not every little detail.

If you want, read your draft to others and ask for feedback. It can help to say your Purpose Statement out loud to someone, just so you know what it feels like to claim it as your own. Think of yourself as a tuning fork for this statement: do the words strike a resonant chord in you? Can you feel a deep meaning and knowing in your statement? A good statement draws you toward it and generates energy in you. It's like putting wind in your sails; you know where you are headed when your purpose is clear and you naturally have the energy to get there. Here are some clues that you've connected with your purpose:

- You feel a strong connection with the purpose you've described.
- You have a desire to fulfill it.
- You feel deep pleasure when you act in concert with it.
- Your interests naturally gravitate toward manifesting it.
- You want a written version of it around you, as a "touch point" that centers you in your daily life.

Commit to getting really clear on your Purpose Statement. The goal is a one- or two-sentence statement that you will remember and say to yourself (and others if you want).

One final note: Your first reaction to your Purpose Statement may be something like, "Oh, it sounds so grandiose! I'm just not comfortable playing that big." Well, let me say this:

You are that big.

And as Marianne Williamson said, your "playing small" serves no one. You are here for a purpose, and that purpose just can't be small. Is it possible that one reason why you've been unhappy in your work is that, deep down inside, you know that you have been trying to make yourself small in order to maintain the status quo? And it just gets harder and harder for you to do that? So now that you're here, isn't it time to give yourself permission to live big on the stage of your life? To step into a place that fits you? I think it is.

Our deepest fear is not that we are inadequate.

Our deepest fear is that we are powerful beyond measure.

It is our light, not our darkness that most frightens us.

We ask ourselves, Who am I to be brilliant, gorgeous, talented, fabulous?

Actually, who are you not to be? You are a child of God.

Your playing small does not serve the world.

There's nothing enlightened about shrinking so that other people won't feel insecure around you. We are all meant to shine, as children do. We were born to make manifest the glory of God that is within us. It's not just in some of us; it's in everyone. And as we let our own light shine, we unconsciously give other people permission to do the same. As we're liberated from our own fear, our presence automatically liberates others.

Marianne Williamson

THE SECOND KEY:
COMMAND YOUR PRISON WARDEN

An old Cherokee is teaching his grandson about the battle that goes on inside people.

"My son, it is a terrible fight and it is between two wolves. One is evil: he is anger, envy, sorrow, regret, greed, arrogance, self-pity, guilt, resentment, inferiority, lies, false pride, superiority, and ego. The other is good: he is joy, peace, love, hope, serenity, humility, kindness, benevolence, empathy, generosity, truth, compassion, and faith."

The boy thought about it for a minute and then asked his grandfather, "Which wolf will win?"

The old Cherokee simply replied, "The one you feed."

Cherokee legend

Oh, that voice. You've heard it, prattling on inside your head, telling you what you're not up to, pointing out how badly things might go, what people might say if you fail, how silly your dreams are, and generally keeping you small. It disguises itself with "This is in your best interest" and "Let's be practical." It asks unanswerable questions that begin with "How" and "Why." It may stand there looking down at you with its arms akimbo, or wag its bony finger while telling you what you "should" be doing, thinking, feeling. It churns out frightening future scenarios that always end in disaster. Worry. Worry. Worry. No. No. No. Stop. Stop. Stop.

Meet your Prison Warden.

It's odd to meet something for the first time that has been living with you for most of your life, isn't it? This part of you has been operating behind the scenes, sneaking around, pulling your strings, and taking options off the table since adolescence. It hides inside you, disguised as "the voice of reason" or "the expert" or some other ridiculous nonsense. It's known by many names in many circles; here are some:

- Saboteur
- Inner Critic
- Ego
- Gremlin
- Lizard Brain
- Monkey Mind
- Resistance

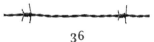

Familiar with any of those? Doesn't matter… it's the same regardless of what it's called or how much you may have learned about it. And here's the deal: it is actually a part of your brain. It exists and operates in all brains, human or otherwise. It's called the amygdala, an almond-shaped set of neurons located deep in the brain's medial temporal lobe. It's a biological fact inside you. Go ahead, Google it.

So is this bad news or good news, knowing that this incredibly small-making, unhelpful, and critical voice is actually the expression of a portion of your brain? Maybe it's both.

Here's why it matters: as I mentioned earlier, the amygdala resides in all brains. It is prehistoric, so it's been around since the beginning of time. And just like many other parts of your body, it has one job: it supports and promotes survival of the species, one individual at a time. There are two primary methods for this imperative: procreation and safety. Ensuring that individual members of a species are generating new members, and protecting existing members from harm's way, results in the continuation of the species. Are you with me so far?

Now that we've had a brief biology lesson, let's get to the heart of the matter, shall we? We're not going to explore procreation here; not much to know about that for purposes of this book! But safety, and the urges that promote it, is where we're going to spend our time.

Of all the species with brains on the planet, humans make up an itsy-bitsy, teeny-tiny portion of the total. And when we look at other species, we see that most of them are either in danger of not eating (or drinking or having shelter) or in danger of being eaten. Fear of Lack or Fear of Attack. *No Lunch* or *Becoming Lunch*. The amygdala's job is to devise consistently effective ways of keeping the individual safe from harm. And the most effective, time-tested way to achieve that goal is through the use of fear.

The amygdala communicates to the cheetah: "When you kill that gazelle, eat as much as you can, as fast as you can, because there may be competition for this food and it may be days or weeks before you eat again." Fear of lack.

It says to the gazelle: "Be aware! Be afraid! Anything unusual, anything out of the ordinary, carries the potential of your future death. You are a walking buffet for other creatures and you must be very careful at all times." Fear of attack.

Wait. It gets better: The amygdala says to all cheetahs not in danger of starvation and to all gazelles living in safety: "If you have enough food, water, shelter and safety, don't change anything." Fear of change.

Now consider Western humans, living in a highly civilized society where the likelihood that we'll starve or be eaten by something is extremely low. Lack and attack aren't big factors, so our amygdala concentrates on keeping us safe by doing its level best to maintain status quo.

To the amygdala, change is dangerous unless it's required for survival. And while you may believe you'll die if you remain stuck in your current career, your amygdala, looking through the lens of primitive survival, sees things differently. You are eating regularly. You have enough water and a good shelter to keep you safe. There are no predators threatening your existence. Your amygdala's job, therefore, is to use every small-making, fear-based trick in the book to keep change from happening.

Isn't that brilliant?

Furthermore, the bigger the change and/or the closer you are to making change happen, the louder and more fear-inducing and insistent your amygdala becomes. It is the gatekeeper that stands, often shrieking with arms flailing, between you and the meaningful change that will bring you great happiness.

And are you having an "a-ha" moment right now?

Fade to your Prison Warden, which is simply a metaphor for the amygdala. Imagine it here with us, the third member of our little trio. Is it sitting beside you? Maybe it's looking over your shoulder and reading these words with you. Is it making side comments, like your own personal narrative of things good and bad, telling you who you are and who you're not? Has it said, "Why the heck are you reading this? How is this going to help you get a job? This is a waste of time and you're not going anywhere. Is it really that bad here in prison? Getting out sure seems like a lot of work. It's going to be hard. And what happens if you fail? Then what?"

Yep, yep, yep. That's your Warden! Isn't it great at its job? It is the King of Reasons Why Not, the CEO of Stuckness. Ambassador of the Small and Settled. You just have to admire how seriously it takes its job, and how well it has mastered it, don't you? Damn it.

> *You will never realize your best destiny through the avoidance of fear. Rather, you will realize it through the exercise of courage, which means taking whatever action is most liberating to the soul, even when you are afraid.*

Martha Beck

With all its being, your Warden believes that what's best for you is to remain small and safe, right where you are. Most of us don't need to worry about starving or being eaten, and our Wardens know this. So they concentrate on the "don't change anything" part of species survival.

There you've been, perhaps many times in the past and certainly now, contemplating meaningful change. Wanting to become larger on the landscape of your human potential, to play a bigger role in your life and in the lives of others. Longing to have an impact. Feeling a deep desire to escape the smallness of Career Prison and break free into a life of purpose and positive impact. And all the while, your Warden has been operating in your brain, churning out fearful thoughts specifically crafted to keep you jailed.

Your Warden has been taking notes and learning how to keep you "safe" (read: *stuck*) for your entire life. It has tried count-

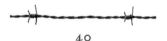

less tactics and made note of the ones that work best. It has amassed an arsenal of fear-based weapons proven to stop you in your tracks whenever you're considering change. Most are disguised to seem as if your best interest is at heart. Here are a few tracks from your Warden's *Greatest Hits* album:

Lack Track:
"You don't have enough experience for that."
"I don't think it's possible to make enough money doing that."
"You're too old to start over."

Attack Track:
"What will others think if you do that?"
"If you try this and fail, you're going to look like a loser."
"You're selfish to put your happiness ahead of others'."

Bonus Track (and an all-time favorite among all Wardens):
"How are you going to do that?"

A Note about "How": If the question appearing in your thoughts begins with "How," you can bet your Warden is behind it. For example, remember now a time when you had a brilliant, delicious idea. One that gave you a sense of who you could be and created a resonance inside your body that felt like all the molecules inside you were vibrating. Imagine that feeling: The bigness of it. The meaning and passion it held. Chances are, a split second after you had this resonant thought, a question appeared in your thoughts.

And it started with the word "How."

> *"How are you going to find a job doing that?"*
> *"How do you know there are even any jobs out there like that?"*
> *"How are you going to make enough money doing that?"*
> *"How will you get the experience necessary to do that?"*

And so on.

Can you feel how those questions just suck all the wind out of the sails of your idea? The way you are brought down to earth where everything is small, safe, and practical? Perhaps you felt silly, ridiculous, or audacious for having had such a dream. Can you feel how easy it would be to throw your hands up and quit because you don't have an answer to those "How" questions? The way they stop you in your tracks? If ever there was an overplayed, overused, devious and manipulative tactic by a Warden, it is most certainly the word "How." I haven't met a single client who didn't fall prey to this unscrupulous, dastardly Warden tactic. Asking unanswerable questions that begin with "How" and "Why" is your Warden's favorite method for keeping you stuck.

In the many years I've been working with clients who have a deep desire—a call—to create meaningful work where they can make a difference in their own lives and the lives of others, I've been witness to the most genius, insidious and malevolent Warden tactics imaginable. New ones are devised every day. And mostly, the same old hits play over and over like an audio loop in the minds of my clients.

The Warden's *Greatest Hits* generally center on three popular fear-based obstacles specifically designed to keep you from creating meaningful change: Lack of Money, Fear of Failure, and People-Pleasing. Let's take a look at each one and as we do, ask yourself two questions:

1. Has this been an effective tactic for my Warden in the past?
2. Now that I see it's just a tactic, will I choose to let it control me going forward?

Lack of Money

> *Money often costs too much.*
>
> **Ralph Waldo Emerson**

Nothing will kill the creative dream of fulfilling work faster than focusing on money. I hear it all the time from new clients: "I want a job where I won't have to worry about money." Or "I need a job where I will make enough money."

Most of us have bills to pay. Most of us desire to have an income that will afford a comfortable lifestyle, saving for the future with perhaps some left over for generous acts to help others. Of course. And let's honor that. We will hold that intention, and I promise it won't be overlooked when the time is right. But here's something you must understand:

Having "enough" money doesn't stop people from worrying about it.

I have coached clients with five-figure incomes and clients with seven-figure incomes. Heck, in my own career I've had five-figure and six-figure incomes. And you know what I've found? The people with five-figure incomes are less controlled by money fears.

I once saw a *60 Minutes* interview with Jerry Jones, owner of the Dallas Cowboys and Texas Stadium. The man has buckets of money. He has never filed for bankruptcy or even gotten close to it. His net worth at the time of the interview was estimated at $2 billion (give or take a couple hundred million). In this interview he spoke of his biggest worry: losing it all and finding himself homeless on a park bench. Seriously. Can you believe it? A man with that kind of money, notoriety, prestige, and power, and he experiences the same park bench scenario the rest of us do?

This isn't an anomaly, dear reader. I see it all the time. Consider the possibility that "enough" money has very little to do with your bank account and everything to do with your state of mind. It can even be said that the more we have, the more we worry because the more we have to lose.

Worry (about anything: money, job security, health, what other people think, and so on) isn't something that is caused or relieved by something "out there"—worry is something you choose.

> *Here's something you'll need to hold in your mind, at least temporarily, if you want to get a good look at your own North Star: External circumstances do not create feeling states. Feeling states create external circumstances.*
>
> **Martha Beck**

Worry and faith are two sides of the same coin. They are essentially the same thing. Worry is telling ourselves a story about the future that ends badly. Faith is telling ourselves a story about the future that ends well. The fear-based story isn't more likely to come true because it's scary, though it can certainly feel that way. You have the power to pick the story. You can choose to place your focus and intention on something creative or something reactive. If you are able to create from worry, then create. And if you're like most people, either paralyzed by or reacting to worry, then I strongly suggest you choose to let the story go. It is a practice. And yes, it can be accomplished.

Again: worry is a choice you are making. Choose differently.

If you're like many people, particularly in light of our recent economic challenges, you may have acquired some debt along the way. And it's possible—dare I say probable—that your situation has been made worse because you've been in Career Prison.

Here's why: think of one of those old-fashioned balance scales, like the ones you see Lady Justice carrying in statues around courthouses. On one side of the scale is *Job Fulfillment*; in the opposite cup is *Money to Spend*. Understand that the more you have of one, the less you need of the other. So if you've been unhappy in your work for quite a while, you've probably been spending more money as a means to attain some form of happiness outside of work. The money and the spending didn't actually make you happy; they just numbed the pain by distracting you for a while. Eventually you find yourself right back in a dissatisfied place, but now you have more debt, less money, *and* unfulfilling work.

So. Are you willing to hold money as a factor that certainly needs to be considered, but later in the process of creating a meaningful career? Money is a Having thing, after all. If you allow yourself to focus on the Being part of you first, and then the Doing piece of fulfilling work, I promise, the Having of money will be much more "balanced." Find the career that makes you come alive, and then turn your attention to money.

Hard truth: If you won't choose to put the money issue down for a while, it's quite possible that you're not in enough career pain to leave where you are. Seriously: does a prison inmate say, "Yeah, I only want out if it's worth it"? No, ma'am. An inmate wants out no matter what. If you've placed all kinds of external conditions on your escape—and money is the number one condition I see with clients—either you are not ready to break free or you don't truly believe you're worth your own freedom. Is your freedom worth it? Are you worth it?

> *You have to make a living; I understand that. But you also have to know what sparks the light in you, so that you in your own way can illuminate the world.*
>
> **Oprah Winfrey**

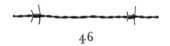

Fear of Failure

Any change involves risk. Inherent in change is leaving where you are for another place that is to some degree unknown. Our human experience has told us that the more we know before we leave for uncharted land, the better the chances we will avoid failure. Our minds tell us that the more data we collect and the longer we analyze, the greater the likelihood that all will go as planned, that "having the answers" will make us safe. This is certainly a favorite requisite to our Wardens. "Just wait. You don't know everything yet. Get more assurances. Wait for a more convenient time. Wait for the feeling of safety before making a move. If you wait long enough, you'll be sure."

Not true.

Risk is, well, risky. By definition it means things could turn out badly. Have you noticed that people who take risks tend to be more confident and self-assured than those who don't? Why do you suppose that is? Do you believe it's because every risk they took turned out well? That for some reason they've got a special chromosome that enables them to avoid pitfalls and bad results? Or maybe they're just lucky?

People who take risks are more confident and resilient than those who don't, simply because they were willing to take risks. Confidence doesn't come from neat, expected outcomes after a risk is taken. Confidence comes from being able to say, "I knew it was a risk, I felt the fear, and I did it anyway." Deep confidence is borne of courage.

> *Courage is not the absence of fear but rather the judg-*
> *ment that something else is more important than fear.*
>
> **Ambrose Redmoon**

Your Warden typically fosters fear of failure in three sneaky ways. Let's look at them.

Failure Fear Tactic #1: Telling you stories about the future that end badly. I call this the "Danger, Will Robinson! Danger, Will Robinson!" tactic (if you were born after 1970, Google it). It's the all-time favorite fear-inducing tool among Wardens. It's the spinning of scenarios that go from bad to worse, to worse yet, to eventually living on a park bench or in a van down by the river. "If you make that change, this could happen, and then this could happen, and then this could happen, and then you'll be a bag lady." It's a cheap fear tactic that is overused to the degree of laughability. Not to you when you're in it, of course, but if you could only see how ridiculously common and unfounded this future-based fearful storytelling is, trust me, you'd cackle.

There are two effective strategies to address and overcome this tactic:

1. **Write it down.** Get the whole sad story out of your brain where it's fuzzy and scary, and put it all on paper (or computer screen). You will find that a fearful story that's outside your head and in front of your eyes loses a great deal of power. By writing it down you will see the bunny trail your Warden is scaring you down. The likelihood of

your Warden's predicted disastrous outcome coming to pass will feel much more remote than when it was swirling around inside you.

2. **Acknowledge the tiny part of the story that is worth your notice.** Fear-based tactics are fearful because they contain an element of truth. It's that minuscule and SCARY bit of truth that the Warden uses to hook you by pumping it up from a small possibility into a certainty. So find the sesame-seed-sized possibility in the scenario and work with that. If that very remote possibility comes to pass, what then? Focus on who you will be and the way you will recover if it happens. You will probably find that doing nothing out of fear is a greater risk than going for it and having it turn out badly.

Here's an example that demonstrates employing both of these effective strategies for overcoming your Warden's future-based fear tactic:

You think, "If I tell my manager that I'm no longer willing to work 60 hours a week, she'll fire me." Eeeeek! So start with that thought and get out the pencil and paper (or keyboard). What happens next? Write it all down; every sad, scary, pitiful B-movie detail:

> *"...And then I won't be able to find another job because every single employer in town will think I'm worthless, and then I'll go broke and won't be able to pay my bills, and then all my friends and family will think I'm*

a loser and I'll be all alone with no place to sleep, and then I'll have to move out of my home with all my belongings in plastic bags, and I'll have to leave them at the curb because I won't be able to find a shopping cart to wheel them around in, and then I'll be living on a park bench, begging passersby for quarters, cigarettes, and pints of cheap whiskey."

Really?? Are you getting the sense of how ridiculous this becomes when it's written down, in front of and outside you, versus when it was running roughshod in your thoughts?

Now let's look at the teeny part that is worth your notice: Okay, yes there is the possibility that your boss will fire you if you say you're not willing to work 60 hours a week. We don't truly know how likely it is—and I believe the odds are very small—but it is a possibility worth considering. So what if it does happen? What then? I'm willing to bet that if you take yourself to that place, you will discover that your resilience and creativity will provide you with a solution that's better for you than continuing to work 60 hours a week. You will feel more confidence and freedom from having taken the risk—regardless of the outcome—than from staying small and allowing yourself to be victimized by your situation and your fears.

*And the day came when the risk to remain tight in a
bud was more painful than the risk it took to blossom.*

Anaïs Nin

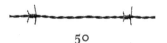

Failure Fear Tactic #2: Telling you stories about your past and making them true for/about you now. "Remember when you were 12 and the neighbor lady got mad because you didn't water her posies adequately? Yeah, well that means you're irresponsible so you'd better not go for this new job because you'll probably fail at it."

If you are hearing a lot of stories in your mind about who you've always been and how terrible you are at certain things, your Warden is having a field day. What you did when you were 12—or even last week, for that matter—does not determine who you are today. Unless you want it to. Your past is a dot on the map of your life. It happened; you were indeed there. Acknowledge it and leave it in your past. If you want to go back and visit, go right ahead. And if you don't, then don't.

The stories you tell yourself really, really matter. To employ a different metaphor: think of your favorite fine restaurant. When you go in, the maitre d' seats you. You look over the menu, perhaps hear about some specials, decide what you want, and place your order. What you probably don't do next is sit and worry about whether the waiter will quit before your meal arrives, or if the chef will decide you're not worthy of what you ordered. The likelihood that you will receive just what you ordered is so great that you probably don't even think about it. What you do instead is believe it's on its way and you wait.

Well, what better restaurant could there possibly be than the universe? Realize that what you say about yourself to yourself

or others is tantamount to placing an order. If you want chocolate mousse, then order chocolate mousse. If you want key lime pie, then don't order chocolate mousse. And for heaven's sake, if you had the key lime pie last week and you didn't like it, don't keep ordering it! Choose to think thoughts, say things, and believe about yourself only what will support, encourage, love, and serve you. When you do, you'll find that the most delicious possibilities are delivered to you.

Failure Fear Tactic #3: Telling you to wait until "the time is right." Something more about your Warden: it loves delay. It speaks of waiting until all your ducks are in a row, or until all the stars are aligned, or until you have enough money/time/answers. It does this because the longer you delay, the more you wait for something outside you to shift, the greater the likelihood that no change will happen.

> *Perfectionism is the voice of the oppressor.*
> **Anne Lamott**

Sometimes waiting is cleverly disguised to look like being busy. "Yes, I'd love to work as a *(fill in the blank)*, and I'm going to need to spend two years in school learning about it so I can know all I need to know before I can begin the career." This is a tricky one because you may have a big Value of being the best you can be at your craft and offering a high level of knowledge or expertise to your employer or clients. This was certainly the case for me when I chose to become a coach. Having a solid foundation of learning and tools and a professional certifica-

tion really mattered to me. It's also possible that the career that lights you up inside requires formal, extensive education. You can't begin work as a doctor, nurse, lawyer, chef or architect tomorrow. That's okay! I get it and I want you to go for it.

However, you may be able to begin your new career before (or while) you're learning all you can learn about it. The key here is to start. Volunteer. Look into internship. Work a few hours a week as an apprentice. If additional training or education feels like another duck for your row, it probably is. If, on the other hand, it feels yummy and exciting and you can't wait to begin, then by all means, begin.

So if you're *waiting*: until you have all the answers, until it feels safe, to look inside yourself, to create meaningful change, to begin that delicious new career, or even simply to do the exercises in this book, you are probably living in a cell created by your Warden. Don't allow your Warden to dangle the key; if you want meaningful work that makes you come alive, you must choose to unlock the holding-cell door and break free in the direction of your purpose.

Reminder: as we explored in the Key Ring chapter, *Waiting* is not the same thing as *Staying*. Waiting involves relying on outside circumstances to change in order to move forward. Staying is *choosing* to remain in unfamiliar, uncertain territory in order to grow from the inside what you want to create on the outside.

If not you, then who? If not now, then when?

People Pleasing/Putting Yourself at the Bottom of Your Priority List

This Warden tactic deserves to be higher than third on the list, but it chose to let the others go first because it is so giving, kind and thoughtful and it doesn't want the other two tactics to be mad at it.

It may not be possible to express how insidious and twisted this line of thinking is. Or how prevalent it is among Career Prison inmates. Off the bat, let's get really clear about one thing: if you are putting the *perceived* happiness and convenience of others first and making yourself last, it is a choice you are making. Let me say that again: You are *choosing* to put yourself last. And one thing is guaranteed if you're making that choice: you will never find personal or career joy and satisfaction by putting yourself on the bottom of the list. Never.

> *Until you are loyal to yourself, you can't be loyal to another person.*
>
> **Byron Katie**

Whether you're a mom, or a wife, or a single woman with lots of friends, you must choose to put yourself at the top of your list if you are to create meaningful and positive change in your life.

"But Amy, that feels selfish," you say.

Here's what selfish is: expecting others to believe what you believe and make the choices you've made. A rose that disdains daisies for not being roses is selfish. A person who attempts

to manipulate others through her actions (including saying yes when she wants to say no, just so someone will like her) is selfish.

Here's what selfish is not: putting the oxygen mask on yourself first so you can be your best and most empowered for those you love. There's a reason why airlines instruct us to do this. It makes sense, doesn't it? Compassion, love, and support must begin with you, or you will never have enough for others.

> *Let others lead small lives, but not you. Let others argue over small things, but not you. Let others cry over small hurts, but not you. Let others leave their future in someone else's hands, but not you.*
>
> **Jim Rohn**

If you're a mom who has been giving her all to her family, you deserve to be commended. Raising tomorrow's citizens is important, even sacred, work. And part of your job is to give your children permission to follow their dreams and live their truths. If *you* aren't doing it, how in the world are you setting a powerful example for *them*? Being a great mom and showing up in the world to do what you were born to do isn't an "or" statement; it's an "and" statement. Your Warden loves "this or that, black or white" perspectives. If you buy into "Either I can be there for my kids/husband or I can follow my heart," then of course you're stuck.

So, dear reader, what's behind Door Number Three? Yes, by golly, there is a Door Number Three. Believe it, give yourself permission to have it, and go find it.

"I'm so busy I don't have time to explore myself/follow my heart/create a delicious life for myself." This is a person who can't say no. Actually, it's not a "can't," it's a "won't." The underlying Warden-voiced belief here sounds something like, "If I say no, then (my friend/my group/fill in the blank) will be disappointed and they won't like me anymore." What an incredible load of manure this is.

By the way, if you're noticing that I'm taking an unusually hard line on this topic, you're absolutely right. Giving your attention to what other people might think is a distraction away from what *you* think. In my work I've found that the most effective way to help a client wake up and choose her own happiness first is to shake and shock her out of her deluded sleep. So I'll bottom-line it for you:

What other people think of you is none of your business. Your only business is what *you* think of you.

Stop doing other people's thinking for them. If you believe other people won't like who you are unless you do what *you think* they want you to, what you really must examine is whether *you* like who you are. You must be your own best friend first. What will it take?

> *It's not your job to like me—it's mine.*
> **Byron Katie**

You have zero control over what other people think, feel, and do. You have 100 percent control over what *you* think, feel, and do. Focus on what you can control. Stop trying to manipulate other

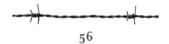

56

people with your actions, including your "yeses." It's fruitless, dis-ingenuous, and self-defeating. Perhaps you've been going along, believing that if people like you, you will have enough proof to like yourself. This is rubbish. There isn't enough external proof in the world to make you like yourself. All of the proof you'll ever need is inside you. Stop looking "out there." Start loving "in here."

My dear friend Shannon uses an intriguing filter to help her decide what she says Yes to. Any time she's presented with an opportunity to do something, whether it's going out for the eve-ning with friends or beginning a new project, she asks herself whether the activity feels irresistible to her. When it's irresist-ible, she says Yes. When it doesn't feel irresistible, the answer is No. And you know what? She's a wonderful, generous, lov-ing woman with many deep, lasting, and delicious friendships. I can tell you firsthand that she's the most supportive, honorable, outrageously fun friend a person can have. When Shannon says Yes to something, she's "all in" and engaged, and it feels really amazing to know that she's present by choice and not because of a perceived obligation to make me or anyone else happy. And she has more irresistible experiences in her life than any-one I know, because she makes room for them by saying No.

Put your "Pleaser" shoe on the other foot: do you really want people to say Yes to you, not because they really want what you're offering, but because they are afraid to say No? Does that feel like a healthy relationship? If you don't believe your friend-ships can withstand your choice to put your happiness first, I strongly recommend you create new ones.

Start saying No when No is what you really want to say. You will find it to be a tremendous act of self-care. And you know what? In doing so, you will give your friends permission to say No, too. Which means that when each of you says Yes, it's from the heart. Isn't that what great friendships are all about?

Love Your Warden

Yes, I know: We've just invested a great deal of time exploring all of the devious ways your Warden keeps you from your dreams, and now I'm asking you to love it?! So here's the deal: have you ever driven through a strange neighborhood, late at night, when the hair on the back of your neck goes up? You lock the car doors, right? Your Warden was behind that.

How about the voice that says, "Okay, that's far enough," when you're stepping close to the edge of a cliff? Yep, that's your Warden. Lock your hotel room door before you go to sleep at night? Warden. Drive on the right side of the road (or left, for you Brits) and trust those coming toward you to do the same? Warden.

Never forget that your Warden's original purpose isn't to fight you or keep you down; it's there to support you and keep you alive. Literally. So it's wise to find gratitude in your heart for it, and to embrace it in its wild, wacky, shrieky ways. It takes its job—a job designed to keep you safe from harm—seriously. Yes, at times too seriously for those of us who aren't going to starve or be eaten tomorrow. And if you allow yourself to appreciate its intent and manage its methods, you can make a kind of peace with your Warden that serves you. It is going to do its

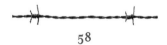

job; you can provide a great deal of direction about "how" it goes about it, what's helpful to you and what isn't. And always, appreciate that in its über-serious and often drama-laden way, it truly is looking out for you.

Summing It All Up

This is what I want you to know most of all about your Prison Warden and the art of effectively commanding it:

- You are not your thoughts.
- Your thoughts are not always the truth.
- Any future-oriented story appearing in your thoughts that ends badly is just a story.
- Fear is not a stop sign. Fear is a yellow light that simply asks you to be aware and awake as you go forward.
- The more fear you feel, the more meaningful the change, and the closer you are to it.
- Big people with big dreams have big Wardens.
- Courage is not the absence of fear; it is the choice to feel the fear and go forward anyway.
- Confidence comes from the willingness to take a risk, regardless of how the risk might turn out.
- The most successful people have one thing in common: they fail more.
- If the thought you're having is making you feel small, it is most certainly not the truth.
- You are not here to live a small and settled life. You are here to shine your light, to put your gifts to great use so that you and the world may benefit.

- Regret is rarely about what we've done. Most regret comes from what we chose not to do.
- Living a big, meaningful, resonant life isn't selfish: it's your opportunity to change the world by giving others permission to do the same.
- The answer to "How?" is "Yes."

SECOND KEY EXERCISES

A reminder: If you'd prefer to have all of the book's exercises printed out so they're physically separate from the reading material and you can complete them on paper, I've provided that option for you free of charge. Simply go to the following link on my web site, where you can download the *Escaping Career Prison Workbook*: www.escapingcareerprison.com/workbook.

EXERCISE FOUR:
INTRODUCTION TO YOUR PRISON WARDEN

What is needed, rather than running away or controlling or suppressing or any other resistance, is understanding fear; that means watch it, learn about it, come into contact with it. We are to learn about fear; not how to escape it.

Jiddu Krishnamurti

Your Prison Warden isn't you and you aren't it. So, then, who is your Warden? Now's the time to put a face, name, and general persona on it. Getting clear on what it looks like, sounds like, acts like, and feels like will help you notice when your Warden is in the room with you.

Introduce me to your Warden. And by the way, it may not have a human shape; some look like gargoyles, some look like lizards, some are alien in appearance, and then again, some look like your Great-Aunt Susan or that mean Phys. Ed. teacher you had in third grade. Write down everything you notice about your Warden; you can describe it in a few paragraphs, or you may have fun ghost-writing its résumé. Be sure to include answers to these questions:

- What does it look like? Find a picture of it somewhere if you can.
- Is it male, female, or something else?
- What is its name?
- When does it show up in your thoughts?

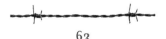

- What comments does it typically make to you?
- What are its favorite fear tactics? Maybe it loves to scare you with the famous homeless-on-a-park-bench scenario, or it worries incessantly about what others think.
- When your Warden is present, where do you feel it in your body? Describe the area of your body that tells you it's there, and the feeling it creates.
- In the past, how have you reacted when your Warden was present?
- What do you appreciate about your Warden? (Yes, really.)

Note: Some people have more than one Warden. You may have a committee of sorts, composed of a variety of Wardens each assigned to different parts of your experience. If this is the case, be sure to write a bio for each one.

Exercise Five:
Your Warden's New Job Description

Now that you're clear on who your Warden is and the ways it has been running roughshod through your thoughts and your life, it's time to put it on notice. No more will it sneak around in the dark and control you like a puppet on a string. Let's be clear: it will continue to try, because that's its nature. The big difference from now on is that you'll recognize it as not you and not true, and you have the ability to manage it. It's out of the shadows and into the light of your awareness. You have the ability to recognize and command it.

Remember that your Warden is a physical presence in your brain; you can't kill it and it's not leaving. But it can be managed, perhaps in the way you'd manage a problem employee who can't be fired. It's time to take the key to your thoughts back from your Warden and clearly communicate what you expect from it.

Write your Warden's new job description. Put it on notice. Communicate what you will tolerate and what you won't. Be clear about the consequences you will employ when it acts out. Understand that fighting with your Warden only gives it power; directing it is a more effective method. Be sure to acknowledge the helpful aspects of your Warden's behavior and differentiate them from what's not helpful. Be clear. Be creative. Be the boss of your thoughts.

EXERCISE SIX:
IN THE PAST/AND NOW

What you say to yourself about yourself matters more than you may have ever realized. If you have acquired the bad habit of saying (to yourself or aloud) belittling, unhelpful, judgmental comments about yourself, it is time to stop. What we focus on grows. Everything you say is an order placed with the universe; your experience will reflect what you express. Realize that when you say something hurtful about or to yourself, followed by a little chuckle or giggle to lessen the harshness, the universe doesn't hear the giggle. It just hears the thought and returns to you more proof of that thought. If you order it, you'll receive it.

It may well be true that when you were 14, you were clumsy. It may well be true that last year you didn't pay close enough attention to a project you worked on. Or that you were obsessed with pleasing others at your own expense. That's fine. It happened. And know this:

- What you did is not who you are.
- You can choose to allow your past circumstances to define you—or not.
- Your past is a dot on the map of your life. It happened; you were there. And if you want to go back for a visit you most certainly can. But if the place didn't serve you, choose to leave it on the map of your past and know that you aren't there anymore. Take from your past only what serves and supports you. Leave the rest behind.
- You have the ability to start anew, every single day.

So, start anew.

Here's how: Divide a sheet of paper in half vertically, so you have two columns. Over Column 1, place the heading "In the Past"; over Column 2, write "And Now." Identify something that you believed was true about you in the past and that you wish to leave behind. Write it in Column 1. Next to it, in Column 2, write what you want to claim from now on. Think of Column 1 as the "delete" pile and Column 2 as the "replace" pile. Be sure Column 1 is written in the past tense and Column 2 is present tense.

For example:

In the Past	And Now
I put my happiness low on my priority list	I am at the top of my priority list
I used food for comfort	I take a walk or a hot bath for comfort
I judged myself for being disorganized	I embrace my creativity
I thought I was too old to begin a new career	I know there is no time like the present and my happiness won't be postponed

Visit this list in your thoughts and actions for several days. Notice the old thoughts that didn't serve you and choose to replace them with thoughts that empower and liberate you. Hold in your consciousness the knowledge that your thoughts have the power to create your life. Choose the good ones. Order up!

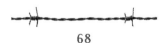

THE THIRD KEY:
CONSULT WITH YOUR WISDOM

*The winds of grace are always blowing, but you have
to raise the sail.*

Sri Ramakrishna

Have you ever felt a call inside you, a pulling or longing
that resides in your core?

Have you heard the "still small voice" quietly letting you know
that all is well?

Have you noticed your thoughts? Go ahead, take a few moments and close your eyes. Notice your thoughts. I'll wait here.

Did you notice them? Great. So tell me this: who did the noticing?

This is your Wisdom. Your authentic self. The boundless, timeless, knowing in you. This is the part of you that knows the way out of Career Prison. Your assignment: learn to hear and trust it.

Be still and know.

In my work, there are three consistencies among almost all of my clients:

- They've lost who they are.
- Their Warden has been running the show.
- They're not communicating regularly with their Wisdom.

This chapter is about the part of you that *simply knows*. It's a quietness, a peace and balance that supports, guides and loves you. Your intuition. She's in there and she will point the way out of Prison. Let's go find her.

Where Your Wisdom Lives

Unlike your Warden, who makes your mind its home and stomps around in your thoughts, your Wisdom is alive and well in your body. You might find her in your heart, in your gut, in your core. When you hear her, you feel her. And when you feel her, you hear her. It's a challenge to talk about one's Wisdom because she is ineffable. She's a voice, a feeling, a knowing. She communicates love and compassion, belief and support. And a soulful longing. What does she long for in you? What does she long for *for* you?

So take a moment now, to get quiet and still again. Take several deep breaths. Gently move your awareness away from your

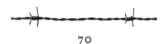

thoughts and place it inside your body. Feel for the divine Wisdom in you. She's there. She's always there. What is she saying?

So let's invest a bit of time talking about your Wisdom, and then I want you to commit to the exercises in this chapter and any others you might find that help you tune in to your Wisdom like a radio station.

I think of the Warden as a loud, obnoxious, manipulative complainer, whiner, and fear monger. She's a finger-wagger. She is the "cheap seats" in the coliseum of the self.

Wisdom, on the other hand. Oh, what a beautiful light she is. Quiet, solid, supportive, loving and yearning. She is your creative self, the part of you that offers deep resolve and interesting, off-the-beaten-path ideas. There is no judgment in your Wisdom. She is so solid and self-assured that she doesn't need to use cheap tactics to get your attention. She waits for you and she is always there when you venture in to find her.

> *It is the still, small voice that the soul heeds, not the deafening blasts of doom.*
> **William Dean Howells**

In spiritual circles, and in nature, there are three places we can be: expanding, contracting, and the place in between. All three are necessary; all three serve a purpose. What's important is the way we choose to employ them in our lives.

We explored the in-between place in the Key Ring chapter; it's The Neutral Zone, the place where Staying is called for. Staying is a crucial, albeit uncomfortable element in any transition from what has been to where you want to be. It is the time when your lungs are neither expanding nor contracting.

Your Warden is the contraction: it is reaction and smallness that can lead you to safety or keep you from your most resonant, magnificent dreams. If you let it, it will remove options from the table of your life so that you feel victimized, stuck, and powerless. It is the pushing out of air as your lungs contract. It's necessary but it need not be the focus.

Any time you are reacting or your career options are shrinking, your Warden is in charge.

Think of your Wisdom as the part of you that seeks to expand, to create "bigness" in your life. It longs for a filling up inside your potential. Your Wisdom asks you to step through fear and into awe. Have you felt awe? That breathless, resonant, wide-eyed place where possibility is unlimited for you? Where you feel you can become the all of who you are? Your Wisdom is the taking in of oxygen as your lungs expand. That new air is filled with life, spirit, and possibility.

Any time you are creating and the career possibilities are expanding, your Wisdom is showing the way.

*You have the power to create. Your power is so strong
that whatever you believe comes true. You create yourself, whatever you believe you are. You are the way you
are because that is what you believe about yourself.*

Don Miguel Ruiz

In any circumstance you find yourself, and particularly the difficult ones when your habitual tendency has been to react, there
is an inquiry you can employ that will be a big help in activating
your creative Wisdom:

"What if this is being done for me, not to me?"

The thing about your Wisdom is that you must go find and ask
her. She isn't going to foist herself on you like your Warden will.
She expresses in and through you always, and you must tune in
to hear her. You must *want* to tune in to hear her. And if you
practice this, you may find one day that you're hearing and feeling her in everything without effort.

But feeling and hearing her isn't enough.

You must learn to trust your Wisdom. She has been offering up
the truth of your right livelihood forever. She has been dropping bread crumbs of experience and grace, synchronicity and
coincidence, guiding you to work that will fill your heart and
activate your purpose. Perhaps you haven't been noticing, but
they are there.

When you look back at your life, you probably see times that felt painful, challenging, confusing, and just plain hard. And yet, now you can see that they happened for your good. Maybe now you're grateful for some of those unanswered prayers. My dad speaks of those times this way: "I was having a good day and I didn't know it."

In what way does all this Wisdom stuff connect to your escaping from Career Prison and finding work you love? Let's begin to answer that question with a hard truth: your Wisdom isn't going to say, "You're right, by golly: this job is terrible and your boss is a jerk. No one should work in a place like this." What it will communicate, mostly through a feeling that arrives when you're not wrapped up mentally in a story and you're not finding fault, is something like this: "The fit isn't good here. This isn't who you are. There's so much more for you out there, a place where you will come alive. Let's go find it."

The answer to your right livelihood won't be a *What*, it will be a *Who*. You aren't going to hear from your Wisdom one day: "You should be a dentist." What you will hear, what you will feel, is a combination of *Who You Have Always Been* and *Who You Are Meant to Be*. It might feel like a forehead slap, a *D'oh!* Or it could be a wave that rushes to the sand, overcoming you in a smooth and overwhelming way. It might be a whisper one day in the shower.

> *I do not at all understand the mystery of grace—only that it meets us where we are but does not leave us where it found us.*
>
> **Anne Lamott**

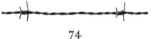

My Wisdom's expression seemed like someone sitting in the passenger seat of my car. It had been there, I felt its presence for ages, and I just hadn't thought to turn my head and actually look at it. And when I finally did, to me it felt like, "Oh, *You*! I know you! Why didn't you speak up and announce your presence sooner?" And then my Wisdom replied, "Hey, cool! Now that you know we're together, where do you want to go?"

When you learn to tune in to your Wisdom, and then you take the audacious leap of trusting it, you will Know. Because your Wisdom Knows. Go now, travel the quiet path inside yourself and find her. Befriend her. Ask her what she longs for. She will offer you something no one else can: A fulfilled career where Who You Are and What You Do are one.

Grow What You Want More Of

Think of your career as a garden of possibility and experiences that you cultivate with your thoughts, energy and beliefs. If you give tender loving care, water, and attention to the flowers in your garden (in other words, what's working for you, what you want more of, and what you're grateful for), you will grow some gorgeous, healthy, lovely flowers. And if you give tender loving care to the weeds (what's not working, what you want less of), you're going to grow yourself some magnificent weeds.

And yes, it's true: even if you give your attention to flowers, an unexpected weed will occasionally pop up. Life in our ever-changing world means the occasional work-related weed is inevitable; that's what makes our experience here on earth so juicy.

What you do with that weed, however, is what's important. You can starve it for attention and eventually it will shrivel up and die. You may even be able to pull it out by the roots and plant something lovely there instead. And I guarantee you this: if you focus on it, complain about it to your co-workers or friends, worry over it and give energy to it, you will grow it.

You will not get to where you want to be by focusing on what you don't want.

Many of us have developed a habit of identifying and naming what we don't want. We're really good at it. But these are the "nots" in your thinking. When you ask yourself what you want in a career, do you find yourself responding, "Not this"?

"Not work where I'm confined to a desk, not work where I feel unappreciated, not work where I'm having little impact." These are weeds, my friend! What are the flowers you want to grow?

"I want work that allows me to be a creative problem solver."
"I want to work in a place where management and peers understand the value of family time."
"I want a career that allows me to connect deeply with clients and rewards me for it."

It is profoundly important to focus on what you want. You are so powerful that you will create more of what you focus on. Want proof? Have you ever learned a new word, or maybe come across a word you hadn't thought of in a while, and suddenly, in a week's time, you hear it everywhere? Or perhaps you decided to buy a particular item; for the purposes of this example, let's say it's an electric-blue Volkswagen Beetle. So you make the decision and you set a plan to purchase it. And as soon as you do, you see electric-blue Volkswagen Beetles everywhere. That is the tremendous power of your mind to create your reality. Use it for your good!

> *The moment one definitely commits oneself, then Providence moves too. All sorts of things occur to help one that would never otherwise occurred... unforeseen incidents and meetings and material assistance, which no man could have dreamed would have come his way.*
> **Johann Wolfgang Goethe**

When you have a positive experience, do more than glance at it and move on. Mark it! Celebrate it! Give it all the attention you can muster. Water it by being grateful.

Gratitude Is the Voice of Your Wisdom

Gratitude is the single most powerful tool you possess for moving from where you are to where you want to be, and amplifying what you want more of. Isn't it amazing that the one thing needed for a resonant life full of love and meaning can be found inside you and employed anytime, anywhere, and you all you have to do is choose to use it? Isn't that the most amazing gift?

> *To live leisurely means to take things one by one, to single them out for grateful celebration.*
> **David Steindl-Rast**

Practice gratitude often. Practice it always. When we focus on what we're grateful for, we can't help but be in the present moment, feeling a feeling that is real and true. Remember that your Warden lives in fearful stories about the past and the future; the one place your Warden cannot reside is in the present moment. Gratitude is always a present-based experience, even if it involves something that happened in the past or may happen in the future. And by the way, if you are grateful for what's to come, the likelihood that it will arrive grows exponentially. Because what we focus on grows, right? It's not necessary for it to already have happened. In fact, you can even assume it's already here and be grateful for it. That's a shift, isn't it? What if it has already happened and we're just waiting for time to catch up? What then?

Is This My Warden or My Wisdom?

When the solution is simple, God is answering.
Albert Einstein

Now that you've begun noticing and hopefully choosing your thoughts, you may find yourself wondering whether it's your Warden or your Wisdom communicating to you in a particular situation. And if so, CONGRATULATIONS! This is a huge step from where you were just a short while ago, wouldn't you agree? It is a great accomplishment to move from being ruled by our thoughts, assuming they're all true and all us, to understanding that we are not our thoughts and we can choose the ones that serve us.

Okay, back to the question of "Is it the Warden or the Wisdom?" Obviously, if you're feeling gratitude, that's clue number one that your Wisdom is present. Remember, your Warden doesn't live in gratitude; only your Wisdom can reside there. But what if you're not feeling gratitude; then what? Here are a few additional clues:

Notice the thought you're having; does it feel soft or hard in your body? Soft is Wisdom; hard would be your Warden. Does it feel like freedom or prison? Does it make you feel smaller or bigger? Is there any judgment of you or others inside the thought? Your Wisdom feels like freedom, growth, resonance, and support. It doesn't know judgment—that's Warden territory.

Are you choosing among many options, or is it "this or that"? Your Wisdom puts options on the table. Your Warden takes them off; it will either say, "There are no options," or construct an impossible decision between only two, where the chance of failure if you pick the wrong one feels really high. Can you see how that would keep you stuck in not-choosing? So if it's "black or white, this or that," go inside yourself and ask your Wisdom to help you identify Door Number Three. It's there. Ask her to help you find it.

Is the word *should* in there anywhere? If so, your Warden is doing the talking. *Should* implies right or wrong, which means both judgment and "this or that" are present. I am a fan of abolishing *should* from our common language; to me, it never feels like freedom.

There is a feeling similar to fear that accompanies a delicious step into something meaningful. It is your Wisdom saying, "Oooohhh… this is BIG and important!" It accompanies a magnificent dream of who we could be if we stepped into this incredible place. My friend and most excellent writer, teacher, and speaker Tara Mohr identifies this cousin-to-fear as Awe. As a guest columnist on Jonathan Fields's blog, Tara wrote an amazing article on this topic, titled "Is It Fear or Awe?" I couldn't even begin to do it justice by paraphrasing. Do yourself a favor and read it: www.jonathanfields.com/blog/is-it-fear-or-awe/

Last of all: If you're still not sure if your thought is coming from your Warden or your Wisdom, then sit with it for a while. Decide not to decide until you know. Wait for your Wisdom. It will arrive, I promise, if you just remain present and listen to your heart. Meditation works wonders here. The answer may not arrive during meditation, but it could very well arrive as a result of quieting your mind and becoming the observer of yourself and your thoughts. Being present, getting off the hamster wheel of daily distractions, and communing with your Wisdom will never steer you wrong.

A Resonant Note

Hearing and following your Wisdom can be a magical, mystical experience. I know it has been for me.

On a warm October day in 2008, I walked to the local Barnes & Noble bookstore and found myself sitting in the in-store coffee shop reading something soulful, rich and exquisite. A familiar

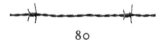

feeling soon came over me, one I'd felt many times before but until this moment hadn't actually paid much attention to. I was reading a meaningful, resonant sentence when a familiar "must share" feeling came over me. This experience had happened many, many, many (let's just say countless) times in my life. Family, friends, boyfriends and colleagues had all been unwitting, perhaps even unwilling, audiences of my resonant recitations.

For most of my life I collected and gave away meaningful quotes the way some people do buttons or coins or seashells; they were placed in a virtual box, accompanied by a joyful feeling that I could sift through them, hold them in my awareness, and give them to others whenever I wanted.

What matters here is this: I didn't realize how important this ritual was to me until that day at Barnes & Noble. Because I paid attention to my heart on that day, I learned that the Doing of collecting and sharing quotes was a deep expression of who I was Being. It didn't come from my thoughts. It didn't "make sense" in the mind-centered way. It wasn't even connected to a well-considered goal. In fact, I collected and shared quotes (and still do) with no contemplation of the outcome. For more than 35 years it was just something that came out of me naturally. And then one day when I was listening, I understood.

On that magical sunny day, "A Resonant Note" was born. If you're not familiar with it, "A Resonant Note" is an e-mail postcard sent three times weekly to hundreds of people all over the world. It's free; it makes me no money and requires a little bit of

my time each week to produce and send. I've never advertised or promoted it. Through word of mouth and a little sign-up form on my web site, it has gained a solid worldwide subscribership, and in its way it is affecting the world. If you'd like to be added to the subscriber list, you can sign up via my web site: www.possibilitiesunlimited.org.

Every quote in this book was gathered in this fashion. I had no idea all those years ago that I would use them in a book I never knew I was destined to write. Collecting quotes was (and still is) one of my Wisdom's expressions; what would come of it never occurred to me.

Your Wisdom is having conversations just like this with you, all the time. She's whispering from your soul and intuition. She is regularly communicating what will make you come alive in your career and in your life. She's pointing toward what matters to you and what will make the world a better place through you. She yearns for work that will free you and bring you joy. Be present so you can hear her: meditate, walk in the woods, paint. Listen, and when you hear, you will know.

THIRD KEY EXERCISES

A reminder: If you'd prefer to have all of the book's exercises printed out so they're physically separate from the reading material and you can complete them on paper, I've provided that option for you free of charge. Simply go to the following link on my web site, where you can download the *Escaping Career Prison Workbook*: www.escapingcareerprison.com/workbook.

EXERCISE SEVEN:
EXPRESS YOUR GRATITUDE

Buy yourself a beautiful journal. You'll find a few ideas for purchasing custom and not-so-custom journal notebooks in the Resources portion of this book, or you can head to your local stationers or Barnes & Noble. Find a lovely one that feels good in your hand and represents your personal beauty and style. In it, write what you're grateful for every day. You can make it a journal with sentences and paragraphs, or you can simply write bullet points. The important element is the feeling of gratitude toward the big and the small things.

Also, you will find that instead of appointing a specific time of day for this activity, it helps to attach writing in your Gratitude Journal to something you do every day. It might be just before you go to sleep, or right when you wake up. Maybe it's immediately after you get out of the shower or before you brush your teeth. The important thing here is to attach it to something you do and not an hour on your calendar because schedules change and we forget. Do this every day for 21 days and experience what happens. If you choose to undertake and complete only one exercise in this book, make it this one. Nothing is more powerful for creating positive change and inner peace than gratitude. Nothing opens the channel to your Wisdom and your values the way gratitude does.

I care so much about this that I want you to write me after 21 days and tell me what you're noticing about yourself and your life. You can reach me via the Contact page at www.possibilitiesunlimited.org. Yes, your message will go directly to me. No, it won't go to an assistant or anyone else. This is your direct line to me.

EXERCISE EIGHT:
YOUR ENERGY BOARD—IT'S NOT WHAT YOU THINK

We've all heard about vision boards: the breathless "It's a miracle!" tales of manifesting material abundance into our lives by pasting pictures of them on poster board. Ferraris suddenly appear in mansion driveways. Handsome men arrive on white steeds to ask for our hand in marriage. On a seaside cliff. While the breeze gently blows our pink chiffon dress. And the violins play.

Yeah, I don't buy it either.

But I do believe our vision has the power to create our reality. The "secret" (ahem) here is not in the things we wish for or in the wishful thoughts we think. The key to bringing your dreams to life lies first in placing your intention (energy) on something. You can create your reality by choosing where to focus your energy. I know, it sounds woo-woo. And yet there's actual science behind this concept. Shall I explain?

Contemporary quantum theory was built on a notion called the Observer Effect. Essentially this idea postulates that nothing exists until it is observed, and that the mere act of measuring (or observing) something changes it. Dating all the way back to the work of Werner Heisenberg, Niels Bohr, and several other scientists in 1924–1927, our modern interpretation of this scientific belief sounds something like "We create our own reality."

In other words, while many of us have lived by the cliché "I'll believe it when I see it," these scientists set out to prove that, in actuality, our experience is the reverse: "I'll see it when I believe it."

Here's something to contemplate:

If there is a $1 million cashier's check in your pocket, made out to you, and you don't know it's there, are you a millionaire?

Here's the bottom line: your energy and intention, when added to your thoughts, creates your reality. It's not enough to think "red Ferrari"—your body must become involved. You must feel the feeling of owning a red Ferrari. What would it feel like to have one? What if you already own one and you simply don't know it?

You see, it's not the red Ferrari that matters at all. What matters is the feeling that owning a red Ferrari will give you. And there are zillions of ways of accessing that feeling without actually owning, garaging, and paying the insurance on a red Italian sports car.

It's not the presence of the thing that matters. What matters is the *feeling* of having the thing; that's what delivers the juice. This exercise is about connecting with the energy of your dreams by using visual prompts. Focus your intention on the energy of something you want (not the "how" of how it arrived) and the energy will manifest.

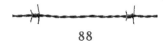

The Steps to Creating an Energy Board

Begin with collecting images from magazines at home, and find more at your local magazine stand or bookstore. This is often the most interesting and challenging part of the journey for me, because I have to answer the Really Big Question:

"What do I want?"

Magazine racks tend to be expansive and organized by subject. Right off the bat you'll have to determine what area of your life you want to focus on: travel? home? career? lifestyle? relationship? A good way to start is to simply wander through the racks and respond when the energy of an image pulls you in.

Once you've landed in a section of the rack, begin flipping through magazine pages. You're "feeling" for pictures here; as you turn the pages, tune in to your body and the feelings that arise from the images you see. Don't try to analyze why you feel what you feel. Let go of your thoughts and go with your body. You're looking for internal responses.

Allow yourself at least an hour to explore the pages of magazines. If you're lucky, you'll wind up with half a dozen or more magazines, each with several resonant images inside.

Producing Your Board

Gather these supplies:

- The magazines you've collected.
- Poster board. (Target and your local craft store are good places to find nice matte-finish board).
- Some fun pens for writing on your board. And maybe some glitter or other embellishment if the playful inclination arises.
- Glue. Not Elmer's (it makes the pages ripple). Rubber cement and glue sticks are good options.

Before you begin creating your board, have a little ritual, whatever feels comfortable to you. You might create a "sacred space" by lighting a candle, taking some deep belly breaths, burning incense, or playing soothing music. Sit quietly and, with kindness and openness, ask yourself what you want. A single word may arise in your thoughts, or maybe images will appear. Take a moment to be with the energy of whatever comes to you.

Step 1: Go through your magazines and tear out the images that create the resonant feeling inside you that I just described. No gluing yet! Turn yourself into a "resonance meter" and whenever your internal needle moves, tear out the image. Don't analyze why or edit for possibility. Include awareness of words, phrases and headlines and include those too. When finished, you will have a pile of resonant images and words to play with.

Step 2: Now go through the images and pick the juiciest ones to place on the board. Feel for how the board wants to be laid out; tap into your creative intuition and allow the images and words to flow. It may feel good to assign a theme to each corner of the board: Health, Job, Fun, Relationships, for instance. Or it may just be that the images and words want to go all over the place. It's important to remind yourself that this isn't an art project you'll be graded on; give yourself permission to create something messy and imperfect. Follow what your body is telling you and try to get out of your analytical mind.

Step 3: Glue everything onto the board. Add writing if you want. You can paint on it, or write words with fun, colorful markers.

Step 4: It's important to envision yourself in this resonant dream. Leave space in the very center of the vision board for a fantastic photo of yourself where you look radiant and happy. Paste yourself in the center of your board.

Step 5 (the most important step): Let go. Now that you've created your board, forget about it. Put it in a place where it can work its energy magic, and where you're not obsessing over it. Maybe under your bed, where you can imagine the energy rising up through you and into the universe while you sleep. Or in your closet, where occasionally you see glimpses of it behind your 27 pairs of black slacks. It's true that some people suggest placing your board somewhere you'll see it all the time, like by a mirror or even on its own special "altar." However, I find

this generates an attachment to the outcome that often leads to grasping instead of releasing:

"Has it happened? Is it happening? When will it happen? Is it not happening because I'm not focusing on it enough?"... and so on.

You see, the important thing really isn't the board, where you put it or how often you see it; what matters is the energy and intention you put into it and the surrendering of "how" your vision will manifest. Place your order and then let it go. It's a challenge, I know. And have you ever heard the saying "A watched pot never boils"? Yep, there you have it.

EXERCISE NINE:
YOUR LIFE IN FREEDOM

This is a journaling exercise that asks you to dream big, in 3D Technicolor. With the prompting of the questions that follow, you are going to access the courage of your Wisdom to create a life even grander than your imagination. Remember the restaurant metaphor from the First Key chapter? Now is the time to place your order and leave the "hows" up to the universe. If you find your Prison Warden providing wet-blanket background commentary as you write, saying things like, "But how would you pay for a house there?" or "No one would ever pay you to be a ski resort illustrator" (yes, those jobs do exist; www.james-niehues.com), kindly show it to the door. You might instruct your to Warden head off to the library to research the history of flypaper or the intricacies of the human digestive tract.

The point of this exercise is to stretch your idea of what's possible and to reach for more, even when it's uncomfortable to do so.

> *Reach high, for stars lie hidden in your soul. Dream deep, for every dream precedes the goal.*
>
> **Mother Teresa**

I suggest you play with this exercise away from your customary environment: somewhere natural, quiet and peaceful, where you have the time and space to daydream. It's important to write down the details of your Life in Freedom. Your dreams gain power when they leave your head and land on paper.

And finally, when you've completed the exercise, consider my favorite prayer to make it complete:

This or something better, please.

Instructions

For each area, channel the most resonant and delicious feeling you can imagine. Write from the perspective that your ideal life has already happened. Allow the possibility that what you're writing is already true and we're just waiting for time to catch up. It's a bit of a mind-bender, I know. Wisdom often is.

Home

Describe the geographic area where you live: the surrounding community, climate, and general vibe. Is it quiet and peaceful? Are the homes close together or miles apart? What kinds of animals roam the area? Is it urban or rural, or something in between? Is there a body of water nearby? Mountains? A city? Fields? What are your neighbors like?

Then narrow the focus to your home. What does it look like from the outside? Is it sprawling or compact? Does it sit on a compact lot with other homes next door, or is it placed on several acres? What kind of landscaping does it have?

Now describe the inside of your home. Is it contemporary or traditional? What kind of furniture do you have? What's the feel of this place: is it warm and cozy, sleek and modern, or something else? How many rooms does it have? What about the backyard? What are your favorite rooms, the ones where you spend the most time? Do you have big elaborate parties in your home, or small, intimate get-togethers?

Relationships

Begin with your relationship with yourself. How do you treat you? What do you like best about you? Then move to your spouse/partner; describe your relationship and what you love about being with this person. How do you treat him or her and how are you treated? Move now to your children (if you have them or want them) and again describe your relationship. And your pets: do you have any? Now move further out to your extended family, friends, and co-workers or business partners. What makes your relationships with them ideal?

Health

Describe your physical and emotional health. What do you do to keep yourself in shape in all aspects of your life? Do you exercise with other people or on your own? Do you hike in the mountains, run on a nearby trail, or swim? Take a Zumba class several times a week? Maybe you have your own team consisting of a personal fitness trainer, life coach, and massage therapist. What does it feel like to be in your body? What's your emotional state most days? Describe your spiritual health too. Do you meditate? Create art?

Work

Being: What is the nature of your work? What impact are you making on others? What values are front and center in the work

you do? What are you known for among your clients, partners and co-workers? What's the difference between a good day and a bad day? What do you celebrate in your work? Describe what it feels like to be you, doing this work that supports, stretches, and rewards the best parts of you.

Doing: What is the experience of your work? Do you work by yourself or with others? Do you have a commute? Describe your typical workday: does an alarm wake you up each day or do you awaken naturally, and at what time? What do you have for break-fast? Do you have a commute, and if so, what's it like? Drive? Walk? Or maybe you work from home? Is your work project-oriented with a beginning, middle, and end, or is it ongoing? Are you on a team, heading a team, supporting a team, or a lone wolf? Do you have clients? Co-workers? Are you delivering a product or a service? Describe your work space. What type of building do you work in? What do you typically wear to work? Do you eat lunch at your desk or out somewhere? Alone or with others? Does your work require a lot of travel, either in town or to distant places? How many hours per week do you work? Is it a structured schedule or does it vary from day to day or week to week?

Having: What are the extrinsic benefits of your work? How much money do you make? What health and insurance benefits do you have? Time off? Do you have a steady income or does it ebb and flow? How much money do you have in savings and for retirement?

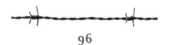

EXERCISE TEN:
GET TO KNOW YOUR WISDOM

It's time to give your Wisdom equal time. More if possible! So just as you did with your Warden, create a profile for your Wisdom. You might want to journal about her, or write a letter to her, or write a letter to someone else and introduce her. Some good elements to identify:

What does she look like?
Where do you notice her in your body?
What does she say to you and how does she make you feel?
What's her name?
When would you like to feel more of her?

Once you've clearly identified and connected with your Wisdom, she will be a great resource in times of difficulty or confusion. When you're not sure what to do, Ask her. She'll tell you. Remember, she's not going to foist herself on you. But when you ask, she will surely respond.

FREEDOM:
WHAT TO DO ONCE YOU'RE OUT

Here we are, Three Keys and a Key Ring later. Congratulations! I'm curious: What's new in you? Has your sense of who you are, the career that resonates with you and what's possible for you shifted? I hope so. Are you "champing at the bit," ready to explore career ideas and options?

This is one of my favorite phases of client work. Even before a session begins, I can feel the energy shift as a client moves from Being to a new kind of Doing. There's a "ready, aim, fire!" feeling that comes from a place of knowing; a stark contrast to the early days when a client *just wants out* and will flail around, aiming darts at a career dartboard while blindfolded to who she really is. "Escaping from" an unfulfilling, soul-sucking career has transformed into "moving toward" meaningful, heart-singing work. Delicious! Are you there? If so, here's my first piece of advice: **Step Away from the Résumé.** It's not that time yet.

I know, I know. We'll get there, I promise. If you even need a résumé (many of my clients never do), it will come later.

And here's what comes now:

Go Explore. Crash Around on the Internet

And what are you afraid of that might work, thus changing everything and opening up entirely new areas of scariness?

Seth Godin

By now, if you've been getting to know yourself deeply, managing your Prison Warden and communing with your Wisdom, you may well have more than an inkling of what type(s) of careers you might like. Has something Big and Scary been tapping you on the shoulder? So big, in fact, that it seems *made for you* and *too much for you* at the same time? Great! Start looking at it. Let it be big and scary and follow it anyway. Google the terms related to it. Just crash around on that World Wide Web and see what's what. *Feel* what's what. Notice what resonates inside you. Remain open to what's possible; don't attach yourself to anything specific.

There is a vitality, a life-force, an energy, a quickening that is translated through you into action... Keep the channel open.

Martha Graham

A good metaphor for this: be a scientist in the laboratory of your career/life. Don your white lab coat and just experiment with stuff. Be curious. When you mix this with that in a beaker, what happens? Does it create a big explosion? Do the elements combine to create a lovely purple liquid? Be inquisitive and open to what's out there and test for the chemical reaction that happens inside you.

Give yourself permission to pursue any type of work that feels like freedom, joy and gladness. Set the "hows" aside.

Allow the hours to pass by while you follow where the Google trail leads. You start with one term, then go look at some web sites; they lead you to other web sites, which lead to others, which causes you to Google another search term. Play in this lab and make note of what makes you come alive. Follow the aliveness wherever it leads.

What If I Have No Clue?

That's okay too. You haven't done anything "wrong," and there's still plenty of exploring to do, just in a different way. The very first thing you'll want to do is revisit your Values Map from the exercise in "The First Key." The list of Values that must be expressed, shared, and supported in your work will be the light that every career idea is held up to.

An abundance of books and resources have been designed to stir up career ideas and you'll want to head to www.amazon.com and crash around there. Treat Amazon like a search engine, identifying

books containing words that resonate with you. Explore books that intrigue you and follow the bunny trail by also checking out "What other people bought" within any book of interest.

One fantastic book designed to generate career ideas is titled *Career Match*, by Shoya Zichy and Ann Bidou. It is an absolute gem. Based on the gold-standard Myers-Briggs career assessment, it is accurate, fun, accessible, and filled with specific examples and great ideas. One of my favorite elements of this book is the imaginary tour through four color-coded departments in a company; each department represents the unique personality/work style of the people in it. This is the ever-important consideration of working in your Tribe! Oh, it just makes my heart happy that such a book exists. Better yet, it will give you specific career ideas that you can choose to follow or not, depending on what resonates for you. When you find a few, go back to crashing around the Internet as described before.

And Speaking of Tribes...

Find yours! No, this is not the incredibly hideous exercise of "networking." Does anyone enjoy spending time in a room full of strangers, most of whom you share nothing in common with, talking about what you "do" and competing with other people in the process of selling yourself? Yeccccchhhh. This is singles dating at its very worst.

Finding your Tribe is an entirely different experience. As with everything in this book, it begins with Who You Are and launches from there. The best way to find your Tribe is to be who you are

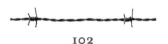

and do what you do, in the way you naturally do it. You're looking for people who share your values. You may find them when you're out hiking. Or attending a pottery class. Perhaps you're committed to the same humanitarian cause. And if you do have some clarity on the work you'd love to do, you'll find them doing that work. Seek them out and engage them. Attend meetings they're likely to attend. The important thing here is to do what comes naturally to you, and more of it. Networking is unnatural. Tribe-finding is what you're already up to, what you already care about, and more of it. Connect with your Tribe in its (and your) natural habitat.

Here's the coolest part of a Tribe: when the members identify you as a fellow Tribe-mate, they will go out of their way to bring you into the fold. They want you on the team! They see you as an asset and they feel connected to you before you ever "do" anything. Tribes are the main reason why many of my clients never need a résumé. Your Tribe is more interested in who you are than in what you've done.

Your Résumé, Finally

Let's begin with why I put résumés at the end of a book about leaving your career and finding a new one, and then I'll offer some suggestions if you find you absolutely must create and send out a résumé.

While managing an animal hospital for several years, I hired dozens of people and received thousands of résumés. I can tell you without hesitation that this is the single hardest way for someone looking for a job to get one. It's a lot like buying a lottery ticket

at the local 7-Eleven, and the odds may be only slightly more favorable. The advent of online job posting and application services has made a challenging situation so much worse. Anyone and their uncle can shoot a cover letter and résumé to literally hundreds of employers with a click of the SEND button. So you're trying to get noticed in a crowd that grows ever larger each day, and your résumé will essentially look just like everyone else's when viewed on a computer screen. The days of lovely linen stationery and interesting, attractive fonts are waning.

What's worse, think of the hiring manager for a moment. She is buried under an avalanche of résumés—often receiving thousands for a single job opening. She has probably devised a system to rapidly weed out as many applicants as possible. This system probably includes general "rules" that immediately send résumés to the NO pile (as in, computer trash can) under these conditions:

- anything with a typo
- no work dates on the résumé
- too many job changes
- not enough job changes
- long periods with no work
- no relevant work experience
- out-of-town addresses
- attempts to stand out that include photos on the résumé and weird fonts
- cover letters that are more than a few sentences long
- cover letters and résumés not customized to the specific job opening and hiring company

You see, when hundreds of résumés come in for a single opening, preservation of sanity requires the hiring manager to carve that pile down to a workable size of perhaps a dozen candidates as quickly—and often as brutally—as possible.

One more consideration in this process is the outrageous cost to the employer of posting job openings with the online services. A posting for one opening to run on the site for just a few days can run into thousands of dollars in cost. Multiply that by the number of potential postings in a year and it can quickly add up to the salary of one or more employees!

To recap: with the old-fashioned résumé tactic, you're competing in a crowd that's never been larger, you're standing out less, and it's easier than ever to put you in the NO pile. This is why I encourage you to find and connect with your Tribe first and let them help you land on the top of a hiring manager's YES pile.

There's no denying it: in some careers the need to produce and send a résumé is real. I believe this is changing, but we're not there yet. If you find yourself in a situation that requires a résumé, here are some suggestions for creating and sending one so yours will perform better than everyone else's. Where creating is concerned, the Internet is quickly replacing the old-fashioned paper medium. A LinkedIn profile is the best "formal" résumé option; people can find you based on the words in your résumé, and it's easy to keep up to date. If you haven't created a LinkedIn profile or you haven't updated it recently, I strongly recommend you do. Go to www.linkedin.com to begin. Ask someone you

respect who has a good grasp of the English language (particularly spelling and grammar) to look it over for you. Few things will kill your job prospects faster than a poorly written profile. It's still very difficult to set yourself apart when every LinkedIn profile is formatted like every other, but as formal résumés go, LinkedIn is quickly becoming a necessity.

If you also want to have a traditional paper résumé on hand, there are scads of resources online to help you create a nice one. Google "create a résumé" and explore all the options. Here are a few to get you started:

> www.resume-now.com
> www.resumecompanion.com
> www.resumesguaranteed.com

When structuring your résumé, begin with Who You Are, not with What You Did. You're looking for your Tribe here, right? So begin with a section that highlights your Values. A Tribe-mate will identify with the person you Are and be more inclined to keep reading. Then go to the Doing part: your job experience, skills and background. If the Doing part reflects who you Are, it will make a lot more sense to the reader, particularly if the reader is a Tribe-mate. And always make sure all parts of your cover letter and résumé relate specifically to the position for which you're applying.

Now we'll turn to the distribution of your résumé. Wow, has this changed in the past decade.

Never send a résumé through one of the online sources like Career Builder or Monster. Have you ever seen the big crowds of *American Idol* hopefuls in stadiums across America at the beginning of a season? The only folks who stand out are the wackos, right? We're talking before they get to audition in front of the judges. If you're not a wacko, it will be very difficult to set yourself apart. And if you come across as a wacko, well, it's over for you. The online application game is almost impossible to win. Don't play.

For heaven's sake (not to mention your own), never fax a résumé. To anyone. Ever. You have no control over the quality of a company's fax machine and thus no control over the way your résumé is representing you. Fax machines are unreliable and finicky, not to mention outdated. If you are tempted to send your résumé and cover letter via fax, I'd suggest you fold them into paper airplanes and sail them out your window instead. It's easier than faxing and just as effective.

If you can, hand-deliver your cover letter/résumé and be sure it is addressed to a specific person in the company. Do your research. LinkedIn.com can help a lot here. Even if you can't find the specific person doing the hiring, if you get close and you do a nice job on your résumé, there's a good chance they'll forward it to the appropriate person. Not a great chance, but a good one. And a far better one than if you place yourself among the stadium of *American Idol* contestants.

Social Media

The Internet and social media are the most valuable and pervasive methods for people to learn about and connect with each other. Here are a few suggestions to make the most of a medium that has woven itself into virtually every aspect of our lives:

Google Thyself. You must, must, must do this and continue doing it on a regular (at least monthly) basis. Do you show up on the first page when you Google your name? Are there any surprises in the search results? Expect a potential employer to Google you, and be darn sure you know what will come up when they do. Now, if you have a relatively (or very) common name such as Ann Jones, this isn't going to be as crucial as it would be if your name is Congolia Breckenridge, but it's still a good idea to see what results come up when your name is searched.

If you have a relatively uncommon name, you might also create a Google Alert that will e-mail you any time new content containing your name appears. It's also a great idea to create Alerts for any career topic that interests you. If you're focused on a career in floral design, create an Alert so you can be updated with news, trends or job openings in that field. For more information on Google Alerts, including how to create one, go here: www. Google.com/alerts.

LinkedIn. As discussed earlier, a current LinkedIn profile is rapidly becoming a necessity for anyone looking to hire, be hired, connect, inform and engage. Employers are shifting their practices of finding job candidates from running an ad (ex-

pensive, wasteful shotgun approach) to searching for qualified potential employees using keyword searches on LinkedIn (free, efficient, laser-focused approach). Be sure to have a LinkedIn profile, keep it updated and use keywords related to the field(s) you're interested in. It's a great idea to have recommendations from previous employers and co-workers on your profile as well. The easiest and most democratic way to get recommendations is to offer to provide them for others.

Finding Groups. People are creating ways to gather in cyberspace to share common interests and new ideas, offer help and ask for help. Look for groups pertaining to your career interests on LinkedIn, Facebook, Google+ and Meetup.com. Join the groups that hold the most appeal and participate as much as you can. One warning here: it's easy to go overboard and join dozens of groups, which may seriously overwhelm you. Be selective, hang for a while, reassess, and continue to tailor your membership to the groups that serve you best.

Facebook. Please, please be aware of how every post you make—and every comment you make to other people's posts—can affect the way you are perceived by potential employers and co-workers. Check your security settings often to ensure that private posts remain that way. Any political, religious, or party-related content should be visible only to your immediate friends. Facebook also offers the ability to create a business page (think personal branding) that is attached to and yet separate from your personal page. You're probably familiar with the profiles where you're asked to "Like" in order to receive

updates, versus "Friend." Those are business pages. You can create one for yourself and place all career-related posts there. Just be sure to keep it up to date and post to it at least once a week so it remains fresh.

AFTERWORD:
TRAVEL INTO THE WILD BLUE

Twenty years from now you will be more disappointed by the things you didn't do than by the ones you did do. So throw off the bowlines, sail away from the safe harbor. Catch the trade winds in your sails. Explore. Dream. Discover.

Mark Twain

I have a friend who was a pilot in the Vietnam War. In peacetime he flew crop dusters over farms in California. It's actually difficult to say which job was more life-threatening because crop dusting is considered one of the most dangerous forms of flying. And not simply because of the pilot's exposure to chemicals (though surely that can't be good either). Crop dusting requires the airplane to skim the ground at a very low altitude. The closer one flies to the ground, the more obstacles there are. Barns, trees, grain silos, telephone wires, and birds all conspire to impede the airplane's path. So while it may seem safer to fly low in case the need to bail out and jump arises, the truth is that the need to bail and jump is much lower the higher one flies.

I had a lifelong desire to learn to sail, and in the late 1980s the opportunity presented itself, so I seized it. What an incredible feeling it is to fly with the wind, the boat heeled over at the deck's edge as it slices through the water. As a newbie sailor, I felt safe in the marina, learning the skills required to harness the wind and water in order to go where I wanted to go.

But out beyond the marina walls lay the ocean. The wild, untamed, deep water. It was frightful to consider leaving the safety of the harbor for that unpredictable place. And when I finally did venture out, one thing became abundantly clear: it was easier out there. The ocean offered freedom of movement and a tremendous confidence that can come only when one leaves the safety of the harbor. I learned through my own experience, and from the stories told by the salty old captain who was my instructor, that the closer one sails to the shore or the harbor, the greater the danger of crashing, capsizing, and doing damage to myself, my boat or the bodies and boats of others.

> *Man cannot discover new oceans unless he has the courage to lose sight of the shore.*
>
> **André Gide**

Leave the safety of the shore, dear reader. Set your compass for the wild blue. Create big, delicious, seemingly impossible career goals for yourself and then turn your sights on them. Yes, it will be scary. Yes, it will feel big, and the potential for failure may be high. Do it anyway. Be the person who dared. Be the person who felt fear and did it anyway. We call that courage, and you are made of it. Put it to use as you create your escape and find your passion. You can do it because it is who you are.

> *So many dreams at first seem impossible. And then they seem improbable. And then when we summon the will, they soon become inevitable.*
>
> **Christopher Reeve**

You have my heartfelt congratulations. You have accomplished a great deal within the pages of this book, I just know it. *Bon voyage* as you venture forward, using your self-knowledge and boundless Wisdom like keys out of Career Prison and toward a career that will free you. I hope to see you in the wild blue, where the breezes are just right and you have all the freedom in the world to be the unique gift you are.

RESOURCES

Suggested Reading

Key Ring

- *Transitions: Making Sense of Life's Changes*, by William Bridges
- *The Art of Uncertainty: How to Live in the Mystery of Life and Love It*, by Dennis Merritt Jones
- *The Power of Now: A Guide to Spiritual Enlightenment*, by Eckhart Tolle

Values

- *Finding Your Own North Star: Claiming the Life You Were Meant to Live*, by Martha Beck
- *Steering by Starlight: Find Your Right Life, No Matter What!* by Martha Beck
- *This Time I Dance! Creating the Work You Love*, by Tama J. Kieves
- *Tribes: We Need You to Lead Us*, by Seth Godin
- *Happy for No Reason: 7 Steps to Being Happy from the Inside Out*, by Marci Shimoff and Carol Kline
- *The Four Agreements: A Practical Guide to Personal Freedom*, by Miguel Ruiz

Warden

- *The Places That Scare You: A Guide to Fearlessness in Difficult Times*, by Pema Chodron
- *Taking the Leap: Freeing Ourselves from Old Habits and Fears*, by Pema Chodron
- *Taming Your Gremlin: A Surprisingly Simple Method for Getting Out of Your Own Way*, by Richard David Carson
- *The War of Art*, by Steven Pressfield
- *The Gifts of Imperfection: Let Go of Who You Think You're Supposed to Be and Embrace Who You Are*, by Brené Brown

Wisdom

- *The Circle: How the Power of a Single Wish Can Change Your Life*, by Laura Day
- *Manifesting Change: It Couldn't Be Easier*, by Mike Dooley
- *Creative Visualization: Use the Power of Your Imagination to Create What You Want in Your Life*, by Shakti Gawain
- *The Untethered Soul: The Journey Beyond Yourself*, by Michael A. Singer
- *Zen And the Art of Happiness*, by Chris Prentiss
- *A New Earth: Awakening to Your Life's Purpose*, by Eckhart Tolle
- *Let Your Life Speak: Listening for the Voice of Vocation*, by Parker J. Palmer
- *The Artist's Way*, by Julia Cameron
- *Traveling Mercies: Some Thoughts on Faith*, by Anne Lamott

What's Next
- *Linchpin: Are You Indispensable?* by Seth Godin
- *Escape from Cubicle Nation: From Corporate Prisoner to Thriving Entrepreneur,* by Pamela Slim
- *Now, Discover Your Strengths,* by Marcus Buckingham and Donald O. Clifton
- *Career Match: Connecting Who You Are with What You'll Love to Do,* by Shoya Zichy and Ann Bidou
- *Make a Name for Yourself: 8 Steps Every Woman Needs to Create a Personal Brand Strategy for Success,* by Robin Fisher Roffer
- *What Color Is Your Parachute? A Practical Manual for Job-Hunters and Career-Changers,* by Richard N. Bolles
- *The Power Formula for LinkedIn Success: Kick-start Your Business, Brand, and Job Search,* by Wayne Breitbarth
- *Social Networking for Career Success: Using Online Tools to Create a Personal Brand,* by Miriam Salpeter
- *Unbeatable Résumés: America's Top Recruiter Reveals What REALLY Gets You Hired,* by Tony Beshara

Blogs and Other Good Stuff
- *Getting Unstuck,* an audio CD by Pema Chodron. You can find this CD at www.amazon.com.
- *Leveraging the Universe and Engaging the Magic,* an audio CD by Mike Dooley. You can find this on his web site, www.tut.com, or at www.amazon.com.
- *Notes from the Universe* by Mike Dooley: www.tut.com/account/register.

- *Experience Yoga Nidra*, a guided deep relaxation audio CD by Swami Janakananda Saraswati. You can find this CD at www. amazon.com.
- Seth Godin's daily blog: sethgodin.typepad.com. Daily posts from one of the great marketing, business, and inspirational minds of our time. If you're looking for a virtual mentor to remind you of the important (and sometimes hard) truths behind business, career, and personal success, Seth just may be your guy.
- *Jill Bolte Taylor's Powerful Stroke of Insight*: a TED talk: www.ted.com/talks/jill_bolte_taylor_s_powerful_stroke_of_insight.html.
- *Susan Cain on the Power of Introverts*: a TED talk: www.ted.com/talks/lang/en/susan_cain_the_power_of_introverts.html.
- *Brené Brown on the Power of Vulnerability*: a TED talk: www.ted.com/talks/brene_brown_on_vulnerability.html.
- *A Resonant Note*, an e-mail postcard sent three times weekly by Amy Van Court. Sign up on my web site: www.possibilitiesunlimited.org.

Here are some great online resources for your Gratitude Journal, customized just the way you want it:

- www.myndology.com. This is an eco-friendly option. You buy the cover once and insert refills of paper as needed.
- www.moleskineus.com. Moleskin has been around forever. Really special leather-bound journals. You can also find them at many local bookstores and stationers, including Barnes & Noble.
- www.cafepress.com/make/custom-journals. These can be customized by uploading your own pictures so the journal truly is an expression of you, inside and out.

ACKNOWLEDGMENTS

The greatest gift anyone can give their child is the freedom to choose. And right beside that gift is the belief that no matter what, that child will fly. Every good thing that has ever come into my life happened because my mom and dad believed in me and insisted that I blaze my own trail. From my mom I gained a fierce independence and the clear vision of what it means to make one's self a priority. My dad gave me my heart and my humor, and he instilled in me the deep knowing that I have always been more than good enough. It is a blessing—and a necessity—that we are free to choose what to believe about ourselves, about others, about the world, and about the nature of the universe. I have always been fascinated by what people choose to believe, and it is clear that many don't know they're choosing. Because of my mom and dad, I have always known I was choosing. And I always knew I had the power to believe something different. I love you, Mom. I love you, Dad.

It was a vulnerable, scary, exciting time when I woke up and realized that my life purpose was ignited by the idea of becoming a professional coach. The one person I felt safe enough to whisper this secret to was my sister and best friend, Laurie. Ironically, because I trust her implicitly, she was also the only person who could kill the dream. Her "Well, *duh*, what have I been telling you for years?!" response blew oxygen on that little ember. I am on fire (in the best possible way) because Laurie sees, knows, and accepts me in the deepest possible way. Even (especially?) when I'm not paying attention. I love you, Sis.

My brother Peter has achieved success in meaningful and lasting areas where I never will. There is no better example of the courage of an open heart than he. When the words *unconditional love* are spoken—by me or anyone else—it is Peter's face, and Peter's life, that I see. I celebrate the truth of who he has always been: someone who has the courage to give and ask for love, time and time again. Thank you for your undaunted love, Peter. I love you right back!

I have a bizarre internal "grace meter" that, when activated, launches me into an embarrassing tear-filled episode. Even the most casual of conversations can set this grace meter off, reducing me to a blubbering fool. With no one does this happen more often than with Tom Evans. I had not a clue how the universe's amazing generosity would collide with my pure dumb luck one Manhattan day in 1990 when I interviewed for an advertising sales job at *U.S. News & World Report* magazine, working for Tom. There is no grace quite like that kind of grace, and every time we talk I am overcome with gratitude for it. The hope I carry for all my clients is that they will be fortunate enough one day to experience the gift of working for someone who leads, mentors, understands, values, inspires and tolerates them in the ways Tom has done for me. Tom, thank you for al-

lowing me to feel seen, understood, and valued so I could create success on my terms.

One of the biggest gifts that came from being hired by Tom has been the experience of working with and for Don Ross. Don is unique in all the world in his ability to travel at a 45-degree forward angle at all times, while being thoughtful and flexible enough to stop midstride and give all of his attention to someone who needs it. Don has the uncanny ability to predict my freak-outs before they happen. Every single time my Prison Warden starts in about how difficult something might be, I channel Don's relentless positivity. He is a person for whom the concept of failure is not even on the radar. Don, you are a dear friend who has backed me at times when it may not have been easy, fun, or convenient. Thank you.

I had no idea how important and soul-lifting a Tribe can be until joining the Unity Church of Fort Worth choir in 2004. For three years, Melinda Allen, Connie and Art Montoya, Terri Smith, John Leach, Sandra Dawson, Kelly Richards, Irene Smith, and many, many others fed my spirit, taught me love, embraced me and provided a soft place to land. They still do. Senior Minister Paul John Roach has always been gracious, kind, and generous to me, every time he could. These people gave me wings and set me free, and I flew away to distant lands. They aren't simply living in my heart; they are my heart.

Another powerful Tribe invited me in when I decided to become a coach. I am overcome with gratitude for the gift of

friendship with Shannon Baker, Tara Mohr, Kevin Ciccotti, Stephanie Lovinger, and so many Tribe-mates on the journey at the Coaches Training Institute. Meeting, knowing, and collaborating with you is why I want every one of my clients to find her Tribe, as I found mine.

I want to shout from the rooftop the names of the two women who took this book-dream and brought it to life. It is a scary and thrilling thing to hand over the heart of one's work to others, with the tender hope that they will breathe it into existence with care and integrity. Ally Peltier, the editor of this book, was a gift from heaven (or the Internet, where I found her) who "got it" from Day One. She provided candid feedback and wisdom that honored my desire to make a positive, meaningful impact on readers above everything else. And then there's Adina Cucicov, whose design of the cover and interior masterfully captured the book's spirit. She met every deadline (from Italy, mind you) while creating gorgeous art in the design of the book. If that isn't a beautiful example of left brain/right brain balance, I don't know what is.

There is a chorus of people who sing the harmony of this book. They are people who have changed my life and influenced what I believe about myself and about the world. And I've never met any of them (in person). In order of appearance: Anthony Robbins, Marianne Williamson, Seth Godin, Anne Lamott, Eckhart Tolle, Martha Beck, Oprah Winfrey, Mike Dooley, Tama Kieves, Marci Shimoff, Pam Slim, Dennis Merritt Jones.

And finally, to my clients: You have courageously shared your-selves with me, invited me in, and offered the great gift of al-lowing me to join you on your journey. Coaching and guiding you continues to be the most challenging, rewarding, astonish-ing, remarkable and soul-singing work I've ever done. Thank you for stepping onto the ledge. Thank you for allowing me the privilege of coaxing you to spring forth. And thank you for the giving me—and the world—the gift of your authentic flight into places resonant and unknown. You inspire every day. The world is a better place because you are being you in it.

ABOUT THE AUTHOR

Amy Van Court's unique perspective on career success was developed through her experiences working in top-flight companies such as *U.S. News & World Report* magazine, *Fast Company* magazine, VCA Animal Hospitals, and Bankrate.com. Her executive and managerial positions in these organizations, combined with her spiritual philosophy and formal coach training, have created an understanding of the goals and obstacles encountered by career women around the world.

Amy is an internationally certified career coach with a deep passion for helping women create success on their terms. She is available for one-on-one coaching, group coaching, and speaking engagements.

Find out more on her web site, www.possibilitiesunlimited.org, or e-mail her directly at amy@possibilitiesunlimited.org.

Home for Amy is Denver, Colorado, with Morgan, her Welsh Corgi dog, and Schuyler, a Burmese cat. She is an avid horsewoman, a fan of sailing and all things ocean, and the owner of a Saleen Mustang muscle car.

Made in the USA
San Bernardino, CA
15 March 2016